NATIONAL STRATEGIES FOR CARBON MARKETS UNDER THE PARIS AGREEMENT

MAKING INFORMED POLICY CHOICES

NOVEMBER 2023

ASIAN DEVELOPMENT BANK

ADB

Contents

Appendixes

Table, Figures, and Boxes

Foreword

Asia and the Pacific is at the front line in combating climate change and meeting the targets under the Paris Agreement. The region is responsible for over 50% of global greenhouse gas emissions and highly vulnerable to the impacts of climate change, such as more intense floods, droughts, cyclones, and heat stress that are impacting millions of people. Women, children, and poor people are among the most affected. Urgent action is needed at scale to help the region pave a sustainable and resilient future for the upcoming generations. Mobilizing both domestic and international sources of finance, including from the private sector, will be critical.

Well-designed carbon markets are an integral element of the broader climate policy architecture that countries can adopt to mitigate climate change and enable the transition to low-carbon economies. These approaches can support the reduction of greenhouse gas emissions cost-effectively, enhance the economic competitiveness of low-carbon technologies by creating strong price signals, and generate revenue streams that can be channeled to climate adaptation and resilience.

As highlighted in the new Energy Policy of the Asian Development Bank (ADB), robust carbon pricing instruments such as carbon markets can be effective in accelerating the diffusion of low-carbon technologies and increasing the use of non-fossil-fuel energy. Carbon finance—mobilized through bilateral, regional, and global carbon markets—can lower financial barriers, enhance the share of renewables in the electricity supply mix, and foster regional cooperation through power trade.

ADB has built strong expertise in carbon markets and carbon pricing through its Carbon Market Program. The Carbon Market Program has evolved in response to the Paris Agreement and the changing architecture of international carbon markets. It takes a holistic approach to enhancing the ability of ADB developing member countries to develop and take advantage of domestic, bilateral, and global carbon markets to achieve their nationally determined contributions and raise the ambition over time.

ADB's initiatives on carbon markets are part of its wider efforts to enhance climate action and pursue green growth in the region. To better address the region's polycrisis, ADB has updated its Capital Adequacy Framework and unlocked $100 billion in new funding capacity over the next decade. This expansion of available funds will be further leveraged through mobilizing private and domestic capital to move from the billions to the trillions required to tackle the climate crisis.

In this context, this publication is timely as it introduces the landscape of carbon market opportunities and provides a framework for countries on how to best take advantage of these markets. I hope that this report will help policymakers enhance their efforts to design and implement an efficient and integrated approach to carbon markets as part of the broader climate policy architecture. ADB remains steadfast in supporting them and its developing member countries to effectively utilize carbon markets in alignment with their national circumstances and priorities.

Bruno Carrasco
Director General
Climate Change and Sustainable Development Department
Asian Development Bank

Preface

Carbon markets are an integral element of the broader climate policy architecture since they can reduce greenhouse gas emissions cost-effectively and incentivize the diffusion of low-carbon technologies and solutions. There is a broad landscape of carbon market instruments, and they can be applied at the national or international level. While compliance carbon markets emanate from national and/or international policy or regulatory agreements, buyers typically participate in the voluntary market for the fulfillment of their voluntary climate commitments.

There is growing momentum and interest from members of the Asian Development Bank (ADB) to take advantage of the broad landscape of carbon markets. Indonesia, Kazakhstan, New Zealand, the People's Republic of China (PRC), and the Republic of Korea have implemented domestic emissions trading systems through which they cap the allowed amount of emissions in the jurisdiction and allow the market to trade emission allowances. Meanwhile, Thailand has a voluntary crediting market, and the PRC has a Certified Emission Reductions Scheme. The main benefit of carbon crediting mechanisms is that they can facilitate the identification of emission reduction activities and contribute to price discovery, while providing flexibility to emissions trading systems.

While domestic carbon market instruments can help ADB members achieve emission reduction targets, international carbon markets can mobilize additional international finance. Accordingly, countries in the region are establishing national frameworks to enable participation in international carbon markets under Article 6 of the Paris Agreement and are also benefiting from the voluntary carbon market. Several countries are engaging in both domestic carbon markets as well as the international markets.

International carbon markets have gained much attention in recent times. The voluntary carbon market has grown to a value of $2 billion, driven by increasing carbon credit issuance and prices, particularly for nature-based carbon credits. At the same time, concerns have been raised regarding the environmental integrity and quality of carbon credits being sold in carbon markets. The market for carbon credits under Article 6 of the Paris Agreement is still in its infancy; however, the last couple of years have seen a significant momentum. Countries are preparing for Article 6 transactions through establishing bilateral agreements and building capacity to implement the rules and guidance agreed by the Conference of the Parties (COP) to the Paris Agreement at COP26 and COP27.

As Asia and the Pacific's climate bank, ADB remains steadfast in continuing its holistic support on carbon markets by providing technical and capacity-building support and mobilizing carbon finance. ADB recognizes that there are both opportunities and challenges of utilizing carbon markets. Therefore, there is a need to support policymakers to understand the broad landscape of carbon market opportunities and develop frameworks to act in operationalizing and participating in these markets. More action is needed and expected, particularly concerning the international carbon markets, which can help ADB members attract much-needed carbon finance and diffuse advanced low-carbon technologies. Carbon markets are most effective when implemented as part of the broader climate policy architecture and in tandem with other policies, such as removing fossil fuel subsidies and creating regulatory conditions that promote private sector engagement.

This study lays the landscape of emerging carbon market opportunities, focusing on Article 6 of the Paris Agreement and the voluntary carbon market, and shares insights on their interlinkages and interactions. The study aims to provide a guidance framework to support policymakers on how countries can engage with the international carbon markets in pursuance of their climate ambition with due consideration of their national circumstances and priorities. We hope this study will help policymakers increase their understanding of the variety of available carbon-market instruments, how the instruments fit in the larger climate policy context, and the ways carbon markets can be designed to suit national climate objectives.

Acknowledgments

This study, National Strategies for Carbon Market under the Paris Agreement—Making Informed Policy Choices, has been developed by the Article 6 Support Facility of the Asian Development Bank (ADB) under its Carbon Market Program within its Climate Change and Sustainable Development Department (CCSD).

Virender Kumar Duggal, principal climate change specialist, CCSD, conceptualized and guided the development of this knowledge product. Martijn Wilder A.M., and Richard Saines ONM from Pollination conducted the research and produced the initial report, which is duly acknowledged and appreciated. The technical inputs from a team of ADB experts including Rastraraj Bhandari, Takeshi Miyata, Takahiro Murayama, and Johan Nylander are also appreciated. This study has hugely benefited from the peer review conducted by Christina Pak, principal counsel, Office of the General Counsel, ADB; Daniele Quaggiotto, senior counsel, Office of the General Counsel, ADB; Mark Johnson, carbon markets business manager at Ricardo PLC; and Mischa Classen, managing director at Classen.

The timely publication of this study was made possible by the valuable coordination and administrative support of Janet Arlene Amponin, Anna Liza Cinco, Cherille Miranda, Rocilyn Laccay, and Ghia Rabanal. Melanie Kelleher edited this study. Edith Creus performed the layout and composition and cover design. Maria Theresa Mercado proofread this study and Marjorie Celis who swiftly worked on page proof checking. Their diligent inputs are greatly acknowledged and appreciated.

Abbreviations

A6.4ERs	Unitized mitigation outcomes issued under the Article 6.4 mechanism
BTR	Biennial Transparency Report
CDM	Clean Development Mechanism
CER	certified emission reduction
CMA	Conference of the Parties serving as the Meeting of the Parties of the Paris Agreement
COP	United Nations Framework Convention on Climate Change Conference of the Parties
CORSIA	Carbon Offsetting and Reduction Scheme for International Aviation
ETS	emissions trading system
FPIC	free, prior, and informed consent
GHG	greenhouse gas
ICAO	International Civil Aviation Organization
ICVCM	Integrity Council for the Voluntary Carbon Market
IETA	International Emissions Trading Association
ITMO	internationally transferred mitigation outcome
JCM	Joint Crediting Mechanism
NDC	nationally determined contribution
OECD	Organisation for Economic Co-operation and Development
REDD+	Reducing emissions from deforestation and degradation and the role of conservation, sustainable management of forests, and enhancement of forest carbon stocks in developing countries
UNFCCC	United Nations Framework Convention on Climate Change
VCM	voluntary carbon market
VCMI	Voluntary Carbon Markets Integrity Initiative

Executive Summary

Carbon markets offer a mechanism to channel domestic and international finance into climate mitigation activities. There is a broad landscape of carbon markets—both at the international and domestic levels—which can be used for voluntary purposes (i.e., for the fulfillment of voluntary climate commitments) and compliance purposes (i.e., to meet requirements established by laws or international agreements, including domestic emissions trading schemes, nationally determined contributions [NDCs] under the Paris Agreement through Article 6, or the Carbon Offsetting and Reduction Scheme for International Aviation).

This means governments have a range of options when considering which carbon markets to participate in and their level of engagement.

Purpose and Scope of This Report

To engage strategically in carbon markets, governments should define the objectives of participation as well as understand the interactions between various carbon market approaches. Countries can either create their domestic crediting schemes to generate carbon credits or adopt (and potentially adjust) international carbon credit standards. Countries can use credits generated within their border for a variety of purposes—depending on the country—including for domestic compliance use (e.g., a carbon tax or cap-and-trade system), international compliance use, or international or domestic voluntary use.

Article 6 of the Paris Agreement recognizes that countries may cooperate voluntarily in meeting their NDCs through the international transfer of mitigation outcomes. When implemented with environmental integrity, Article 6 can help accelerate investments in climate mitigation and raise overall ambition. Parties have agreed on key aspects of the guidance and rules for operationalizing Article 6, providing clarity on implementation elements and paving the way for countries to cooperate voluntarily through bilateral arrangements. With this guidance and set of rules agreed, countries must now turn to building the necessary national frameworks and processes to facilitate international cooperation under Article 6. However, they must do so while recognizing the interlinkages of cooperative approaches under Article 6 with their climate ambitions, such as the achievement of NDC targets as well as other carbon market opportunities including domestic carbon pricing mechanisms and the voluntary carbon market (VCM).

For many countries, participation in international approaches under Article 6 will require new domestic regulations and legal frameworks to support compliance with the Article 6 guidance and rules. Participation will also require countries to weigh up several considerations, including the impact of participation on the long-term achievement of their NDC. This will require a decision-making framework to determine which mitigation outcomes to authorize for international trade as well as administrative capabilities to facilitate credit authorization. While VCMs typically run independently of government regulation, VCMs have always existed in the context of national legal and regulatory frameworks, and governments may consider what actions can be taken to support or constrain VCM activities in their jurisdiction.

This study aims to assist the Asian Development Bank's developing member countries in developing and operationalizing their strategies for engaging with carbon markets as part of NDC implementation through the development of a guidance framework. The study provides an overview as of 2023 of the landscape of carbon markets and considers pathways for governments to participate in those markets. The guidance framework outlines the legal and policy frameworks required for operationalizing Article 6 to aid countries as they develop their carbon market engagement strategies. This study focuses primarily on the market-based approaches under Articles 6.2 and 6.4 and does not address nonmarket-based approaches under Article 6.8.

Guidance Framework to Inform Country Engagement with Carbon Markets

As countries seek to implement their NDCs and engage with carbon markets, including international cooperation under Article 6, they should address the following strategic elements and operational requirements:

Strategic Elements

(i)   Establish a strategy to achieve the NDC that a government, institutions, and civil society consult on and support. Identify priorities that consider specific country circumstances and development needs and develop a workable road map of policy instruments and finance required to implement the long-term strategy.

(ii)   Establish a carbon market strategy with clear objectives for country engagement with carbon markets and consideration of the extent to which the country intends to engage in international cooperation under Article 6; the use of domestic versus international markets; and the role of VCMs as well as any national regulatory or taxation requirements, including those that apply to international transfers under Article 6.

(iii) Considering the established long-term strategy, develop strategic objectives to underpin engagement with Article 6 including guiding principles and criteria for mitigation outcomes to be eligible for international transfer. Principles should also include approaches to ensure international carbon finance is used toward sectors that are otherwise difficult for the country to finance and means to maximize benefits to the country from the sale and international transfer of mitigation outcomes, such as appropriate use and sharing of that revenue among beneficiaries.

Operational Requirements

(i)   Establish clear processes for authorizing the international transfer of mitigation outcomes and the timing for such authorization.

(ii)   Formalize the allocation of roles and responsibilities across government upon cross-ministerial consultation to operationalize Article 6, ensuring appropriate governance structures and safeguards are put in place and decision-making processes are as streamlined as possible.

(iii) Develop processes for approving the transition of projects from the Clean Development Mechanism to the Article 6.4 mechanism in line with the processes to be developed and adopted by the Conference of the Parties serving as the Meeting of the Parties of the Paris Agreement.

(iv)   Establish clear contact points for the negotiation and conclusion of bilateral Article 6.2 agreements, as well as relevant interministerial or interagency approval processes.

(v)   Establish the accounting and reporting capability and infrastructure to meet the requirements of Article 6.

(vi)   Although not strictly within the remit of Article 6, establish guidance on claims that can be made by voluntary purchasers of mitigation outcomes generated in the country. This guidance should seek to align with the positions promulgated by key carbon market integrity initiatives such as the Voluntary Carbon Markets Integrity Initiative and the Integrity Council for the Voluntary Carbon Market.

(vii)   Align Article 6 transactions with domestic emissions pricing or trading schemes, as appropriate (for example where domestic emissions trading systems are linked internationally).

It would be prudent for countries to develop an Article 6 policy that covers these issues to provide clarity among government stakeholders and international players, including private sector players looking to transact. Countries should use this guidance framework in concert with the Article 6 guidance and rules agreed at the 26th and 27th United Nations Climate Change Conferences of the Parties (COP26 and COP27), subsequent decisions, and other blueprints when seeking to operationalize Article 6. The considerations covered in this report aim to provide clarity on the foundational requirements for a country to engage in carbon markets, as well as options for participation in carbon markets to reflect national contexts and circumstances.

1 Introduction

There is strong interest from countries globally in utilizing carbon markets to finance low-carbon development opportunities. Carbon market mechanisms enable participating entities to trade greenhouse gas (GHG) emission reductions and removal units. There is a broad landscape of carbon market opportunities that is available for countries and the private sector to utilize. Carbon market instruments, mechanisms, and schemes can be implemented internationally or domestically (i.e., across or within countries). Buyers of unitized mitigation outcomes drive trade in carbon markets. Buyers can participate in these markets for voluntary purposes (i.e., for the fulfillment of voluntary climate commitments) and compliance purposes (i.e., to meet requirements established by laws or international agreements including domestic emissions trading systems [ETS], nationally determined contributions [NDCs] under the Paris Agreement through Article 6, or the Carbon Offsetting and Reduction Scheme for International Aviation [CORSIA]). Figure 1 visualizes this broad categorization of carbon markets.

Figure 1: Broad Landscape of Carbon Market Instruments

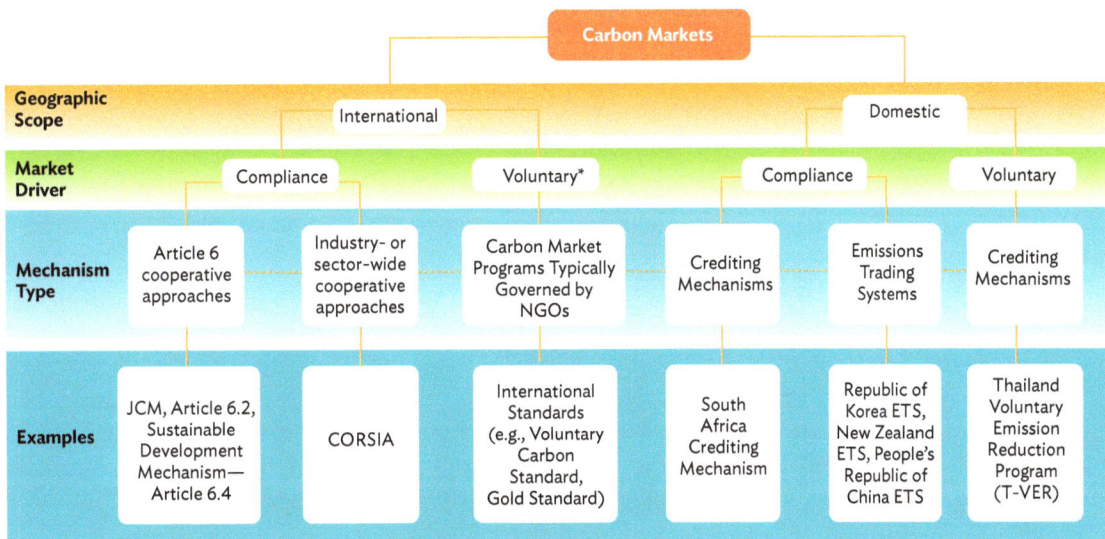

	Carbon Markets				
Geographic Scope	International			Domestic	
Market Driver	Compliance	Voluntary*		Compliance	Voluntary
Mechanism Type	Article 6 cooperative approaches	Industry- or sector-wide cooperative approaches	Carbon Market Programs Typically Governed by NGOs	Crediting Mechanisms	Emissions Trading Systems	Crediting Mechanisms
Examples	JCM, Article 6.2, Sustainable Development Mechanism—Article 6.4	CORSIA	International Standards (e.g., Voluntary Carbon Standard, Gold Standard)	South Africa Crediting Mechanism	Republic of Korea ETS, New Zealand ETS, People's Republic of China ETS	Thailand Voluntary Emission Reduction Program (T-VER)

CORSIA = Carbon Offsetting and Reduction Scheme for International Aviation, ER = emission reduction, ETS = emissions trading system, JCM = Joint Crediting Mechanism, NGO = nongovernment organization, T-VER = Thailand-Voluntary Emission Reduction Program.

Note: This figure has been made for illustrative purposes to gain a preliminary understanding of the broad landscape of carbon market instruments that are available as of 2023. This is a simplified version, and it is to be noted that there are potential overlaps between these markets.

[a] Article 6.4ERs and internationally transferred mitigation outcomes may be purchased and used by voluntary buyers if desired.

Source: Figure developed for this report by the Asian Development Bank.

International compliance markets can be further grouped into two categories: cooperative approaches and industry- or sector-wide approaches. The main difference between the two is the extent of control that the approach imposes on the market. In general, cooperative approaches are linked to the implementation of NDC targets that are established for an entire economy or specific sectors within an economy. They do not impose targets on individual entities. A common example of cooperative approaches is internationally transferred mitigation outcomes (ITMOs) under Article 6 of the Paris Agreement such as bilateral mechanisms under the Joint Crediting Mechanism (JCM). There are also new mechanisms that are emerging that can be best described as industry- or sector-wide cooperative approaches. This includes CORSIA, the first international scheme offering a harmonized approach to using carbon markets to reduce emissions from all entities operating within a specific subsector of the global economy.

International voluntary markets can be utilized by organizations, typically in the private sector, to support in achieving mitigation outcomes, such as in pursuit of carbon neutrality or net-zero pledges. These buyers' targets and use of carbon markets are self-imposed and non-binding (i.e., they do not involve obligations that require certain mitigation actions to be taken). Activity in this context is referred to collectively as the voluntary carbon market (VCM). The VCM is not centrally governed or operated. Most VCM trade is international. Trade occurs in business-to-business transactions and through commodity exchanges and exchange-traded funds.

Domestic Carbon Markets

Many countries are developing or have developed their domestic carbon markets that support decarbonization efforts in their own country and throughout their regions. Domestic compliance markets typically refer to ETS or a combination of both an ETS and a carbon tax, and in some cases, domestic crediting mechanisms are introduced to create flexibility for regulated entities. Domestic crediting mechanisms can also be voluntary and not linked to a carbon pricing mechanism, such as the Thailand Voluntary Emission Reduction Program (T-VER).

An ETS is one example of a domestic carbon pricing mechanism. It is different from a crediting mechanism in that it is a market mechanism that sets a cap for emissions in a sector or several sectors and allows regulated entities to buy and sell these emissions (as permits or allowances) among themselves to stay under the cap. The traded commodity in an ETS is referred to as an emissions allowance. One allowance represents the right to emit 1 metric ton of carbon dioxide equivalent. Allowances are allocated by a governing agency to regulated entities— usually annually—either for free or through auctions. A regulated entity whose emissions exceed its annual emissions allowance is normally charged a fee for noncompliance. Regulated entities trade allowances among themselves to avoid fees.

There are linkages and overlaps within this broad landscape of carbon market instruments, and domestic markets can impact supply and demand dynamics in international carbon markets and VCMs. Specifically, there are linkages between international voluntary and compliance markets, which this paper will expand upon further.

Key Considerations for Governments

Country NDCs will influence decisions regarding the use of carbon markets. Countries will need to take a strategic approach and strike a balance between attracting additional carbon finance through the sale of ITMOs under Article 6 of the Paris Agreement and ensuring that they can finance and meet their own NDC targets, as well as ratchet ambition.

To engage strategically in carbon markets, governments should define the objectives of participation as well as understand the interactions between various carbon market approaches. Domestic mechanisms may require new regulations and legal frameworks. Participation in international carbon markets will ultimately require an Article 6 policy framework to determine which mitigation outcomes to authorize for international trade as well as administrative capabilities to facilitate credit authorization and corresponding adjustment. Governments may consider what actions can be taken to support or constrain voluntary market activities within their jurisdiction or may even regulate such markets.

This report aims to assist the Asian Development Bank's developing member countries in developing their strategic engagement with the carbon market through the development of a guidance framework. To do so, this report provides an overview of the landscape of carbon markets and considers pathways for government participation in those markets. The guidance framework then outlines the legal and policy frameworks required for operationalizing carbon markets through the cooperative approaches under Article 6—focusing on Articles 6.2 and 6.4—to aid countries as they develop their carbon market engagement strategies while exploring linkages with other international market opportunities under the VCM and CORSIA, which are referred to as other international mitigation purposes.[1]

---

[1] Article 6.8 recognizes the importance of nonmarket approaches to help countries implement their NDC. However, nonmarket approaches do not involve the transfer of mitigation outcomes and are therefore not considered further in this report.

2 The Landscape of International Carbon Market Instruments

International Carbon Markets under Article 6 of the Paris Agreement

International cooperation under Article 6 can help buying countries to deliver their NDC goals in a cost-effective way and selling countries to raise funds to finance their own NDC achievement. Cooperation under the Paris Agreement can accelerate investments in mitigation and raise overall climate ambition. Article 6 of the Paris Agreement allows countries to authorize and internationally transfer mitigation outcomes for use toward a purchasing party's NDC achievement or for other mitigation purposes. Countries around the world have different abatement costs due to their exposure to renewable and fossil resources, access to green technologies, or capacity to store carbon in forests or geological sinks that accumulate and store carbon for an indefinite period and thereby removes carbon dioxide from the atmosphere.

Countries that can abate emissions beyond their NDC more cost-effectively than the global average are more likely to become sellers of mitigation outcomes, and countries that have high abatement costs under their NDC are more likely to become buyers. The implication of this is that developed countries with relatively low emissions mitigation potential can finance mitigation opportunities in developing countries and count those mitigation outcomes toward their NDCs. This has been reflected in Article 6.2 transactions to date, with finance generally flowing from developed to developing countries. International carbon markets can enable the effective use of resources; enhancement of overall ambition; and sourcing of additional financing for development; climate change mitigation; and adaptation purposes.

Compared to countries independently achieving their NDC, this international cooperation can reduce the total costs of achieving individual NDCs and, potentially, facilitate additional mitigation beyond the current NDC ambition. Researchers have quantified these benefits using global macroeconomic analysis models and comparing results between independent mitigation efforts and cooperative mitigation efforts.[2] Studies suggest the potential economic benefits of Article 6 cooperation are significant. A study by the International Emissions Trading Association (IETA) in collaboration with the University of Maryland estimates that cooperative implementation under Article 6 can reduce the mitigation costs of achieving NDCs by 63% by 2030, with financial benefits of $250 billion per year. If these estimated cost savings are reinvested into additional mitigation, then the world could further increase the current ambition of NDCs at the same costs as independent implementation in the absence of Article 6.[3] The Environmental Defense Fund conducted a similar analysis, finding that reinvesting the full cost savings potentially achievable via Article 6 into greater emissions reductions could double global climate ambition without additional cost, with half of that doubling coming from natural climate solutions, including reducing emissions from deforestation and degradation and the role of conservation,

---

[2] Most studies on the economic benefits of Article 6 use the Global Change Assessment Model (GCAM), a global integrated assessment model representing and linking economic, energy, and land-use analysis.

[3] International Emissions Trading Association (IETA), University of Maryland, and CPLC. 2019. The Economic Potential of Article 6 of the Paris Agreement and Implementation Challenges. Washington, DC.

sustainable management of forests, and enhancement of forest carbon stocks in developing countries (REDD+) (Figure 2).[4] A meta study by researchers from the Kiel Institute for the World Economy and the Organisation for Economic Co-operation and Development (OECD) found that most research estimates the cost reduction at 58%–63%.[5] Box 1 highlights the potential benefits of Article 6 cooperation, specifically for countries in Asia and the Pacific.

Figure 2: Emissions Reductions from Market Scenarios Relative to Current Policies, with and without Forests
(Total Emissions Reductions from 2020–2035 in billion tons CO_2e)

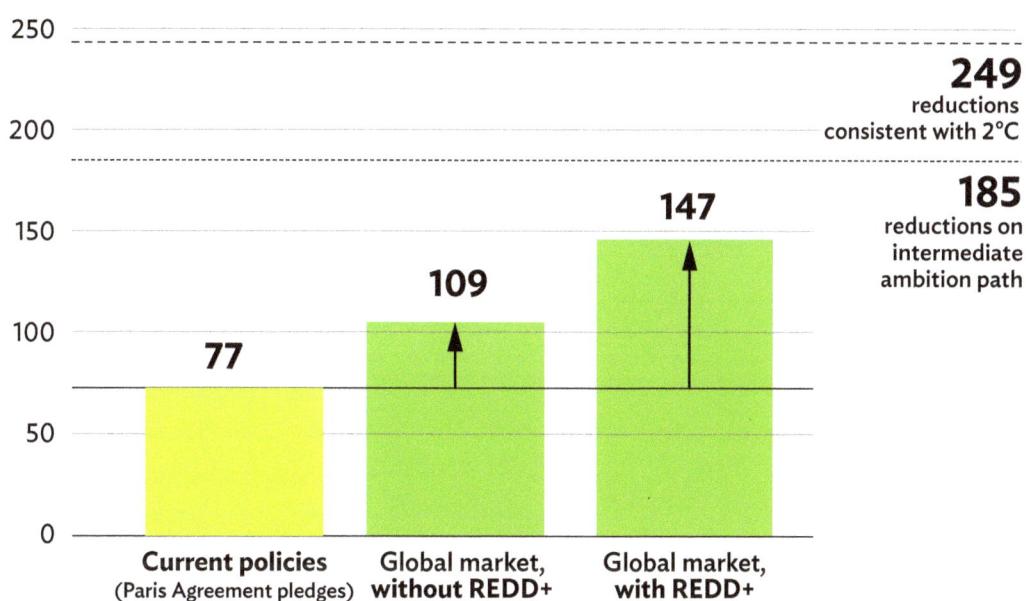

C = Celsius; CO_2e = carbon dioxide emissions equivalent; REDD+ = reducing emissions from deforestation and degradation and the role of conservation, sustainable management of forests, and enhancement of forest carbon stocks in developing countries.
Source: Environmental Defense Fund. 2018. The power of markets to increase ambition—Evidence supports efforts to realize the promise of Paris.

Article 6 of the Paris Agreement recognizes that countries may cooperate voluntarily in the implementation of their NDCs. At the United Nations Framework Convention on Climate Change (UNFCCC) 26th Conference of the Parties (COP26) in November 2021, parties to the Paris Agreement adopted guidance on cooperative approaches referred to in Article 6.2, and rules, modalities, and procedures for the mechanism established in Article 6.4.[6] Article 6 guidance and rules were further elaborated during COP27, with additional work to continue under the negotiations.[7]

---

[4]   P. P. Cabezas, R. Lubowski, and G. Leslie. 2019. Estimating the Power of International Carbon Markets to Increase Global Climate Ambition.
[5]   S. Thube et al. 2021. The Economic and Environmental Benefits from International Co-ordination on Carbon Pricing: A Review of Economic Modelling Studies. *Environmental Research Letters*. 16 (11).
[6]   United Nations Framework Convention on Climate Change (UNFCCC), Conference of the Parties serving as the meeting of the Parties to the Paris Agreement (CMA). 2021. Decision 2/CMA.3, Guidance on Cooperative Approaches Referred to in Article 6, paragraph 2, of the Paris Agreement; and UNFCCC, CMA. 2021. Decision 3/CMA.3, Rules, Modalities and Procedures for the Mechanism Established by Article 6, paragraph 4, of the Paris Agreement.
[7]   UNFCCC, CMA. 2022. Decision 6/CMA.4, Matters Relating to Cooperative Approaches Referred to in Article 6, paragraph 2, of the Paris Agreement; and UNFCCC, CMA. 2022. Decision 7/CMA.4, Guidance on the Mechanism Established by Article 6, paragraph 4, of the Paris Agreement.

Box 1: Potential Benefits of Article 6 Cooperation for Countries in Asia and the Pacific

The potential benefits Article 6 may offer countries in Asia and the Pacific will depend upon whether the country is positioned to be a buyer or seller of mitigation outcomes. Under a global carbon market to achieve nationally determined contributions as modeled by the International Emissions Trading Association (IETA), India, Pakistan, South Asia, and Southeast Asia are projected to be some of the largest sellers of credits, resulting in large financial transfers.[a] Cumulatively by 2050, those countries or regions could sell approximately 4 gigatons of carbon dioxide equivalent, which is more than 10% of 2023 annual global emissions and could be worth more than $40 billion. Central Asia and other Asian and Pacific island countries are projected buyers of credits. The People's Republic of China is projected to transition from a large seller into a large buyer after 2050.[b]

Asian and Pacific island countries may seek to leverage the opportunities for international cooperation offered by Article 6 to attract international finance for mitigation outcomes. This capital could finance economic development and, potentially, structural shifts in their economies toward lower emissions and environmental impact; for example, through the development of renewable energy.

Note: These results are derived from macroeconomic analysis models. Such analysis helps provide a sense of the order of magnitude of the potential trade flows but is not sufficiently granular to inform country-level decision-making.

[a] Joint Global Change Research Institute. The Global Change Analysis Model (GCAM) v6 Documentation: GCAM Model Overview.

[b] IETA, University of Maryland, and CPLC. 2019. The Economic Potential of Article 6 of the Paris Agreement and Implementation Challenges. September

Source: Asian Development Bank.

The COP26 decision related to Article 6.2 established requirements and guidance for the authorization of the use and transfer of ITMOs "for use toward an NDC" or "for use for international purposes other than achievement of an NDC."[8] Figure 3 demonstrates the pathways for treating and using a mitigation outcome under the Paris Agreement.

While key aspects of the Article 6 guidance and rules are still being developed, COP27 provided progress on important elements, including among other things:

(i)   For Article 6.2: reporting, technical expert review, and infrastructure; and

(ii)   For Article 6.4: transition of Clean Development Mechanism (CDM) activities, use of certified emissions reductions (CERs), use of Article 6.4 emission reductions (A6.4ERs), and rates for administrative expenses (e.g., registration and issuance).

The information submitted by the participating parties on a cooperative approach will be reviewed by an Article 6 technical expert review team, which will then prepare a report on its review with recommendations to the participating party on how to improve consistency with the guidance and decisions of the Conference of the Parties serving as the Meeting of the Parties of the Paris Agreement (CMA), including on how to address inconsistencies in quantified information.[9]

----

[8]   UNFCCC, CMA. 2021. Decision 2/CMA.3, Guidance on Cooperative Approaches Referred to in Article 6, paragraph 2, of the Paris Agreement. Annex, para. 1.

[9]   ICAT. 2023. Transparency for cooperative approaches under the Paris Agreement: A guide to navigating the links between Articles 6 and 13.

Figure 3: Treatment and Use of a Mitigation Outcome under the Paris Agreement

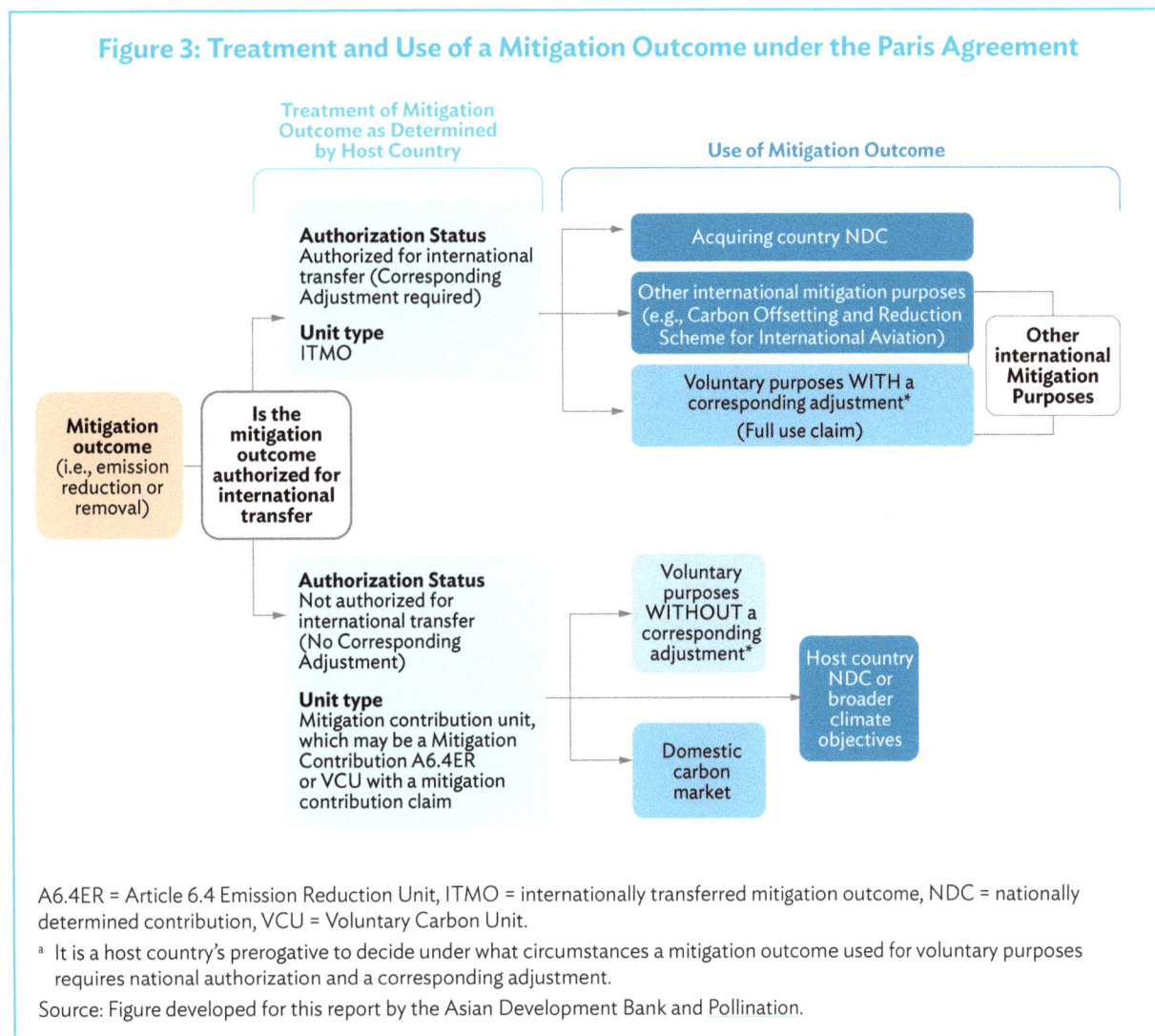

Treatment of Mitigation Outcome as Determined by Host Country

Use of Mitigation Outcome

Mitigation outcome (i.e., emission reduction or removal)

Is the mitigation outcome authorized for international transfer

Authorization Status Authorized for international transfer (Corresponding Adjustment required)

Unit type ITMO

- Acquiring country NDC
- Other international mitigation purposes (e.g., Carbon Offsetting and Reduction Scheme for International Aviation)
- Voluntary purposes WITH a corresponding adjustment* (Full use claim)

Other international Mitigation Purposes

Authorization Status Not authorized for international transfer (No Corresponding Adjustment)

Unit type Mitigation contribution unit, which may be a Mitigation Contribution A6.4ER or VCU with a mitigation contribution claim

- Voluntary purposes WITHOUT a corresponding adjustment*
- Domestic carbon market

Host country NDC or broader climate objectives

A6.4ER = Article 6.4 Emission Reduction Unit, ITMO = internationally transferred mitigation outcome, NDC = nationally determined contribution, VCU = Voluntary Carbon Unit.

a   It is a host country's prerogative to decide under what circumstances a mitigation outcome used for voluntary purposes requires national authorization and a corresponding adjustment.

Source: Figure developed for this report by the Asian Development Bank and Pollination.

Avoidance of Double Counting

Article 6 requires that countries apply robust accounting measures to ensure the avoidance of double counting (a key pillar of Article 6) through the application of a corresponding adjustment. A corresponding adjustment involves a process whereby countries adjust their carbon accounting at fixed intervals to reconcile mitigation outcomes imported and exported. This step requires an exporting country to add back to its inventory the volume of mitigation outcomes transferred and an importing country that uses the mitigation outcomes for its NDC achievement to subtract the same amount from its NDC balance.

This approach prevents two countries from separately counting the same mitigation outcomes, which is required regardless of whether the mitigation outcome falls within the scope of the exporting country's NDC.[10] The process of applying a corresponding adjustment is shown in Figure 4. The avoidance of double counting is also supported by requirements under Article 4 of the Paris Agreement for parties to promote environmental integrity, transparency, accuracy, completeness, comparability, and consistency.

---

10   Corresponding adjustments made for emissions that occur outside of the NDC are added to a host country's NDC-covered emissions.

Figure 4: Corresponding Adjustment Is Made by Country A after It Transfers Emission Reductions to Country B

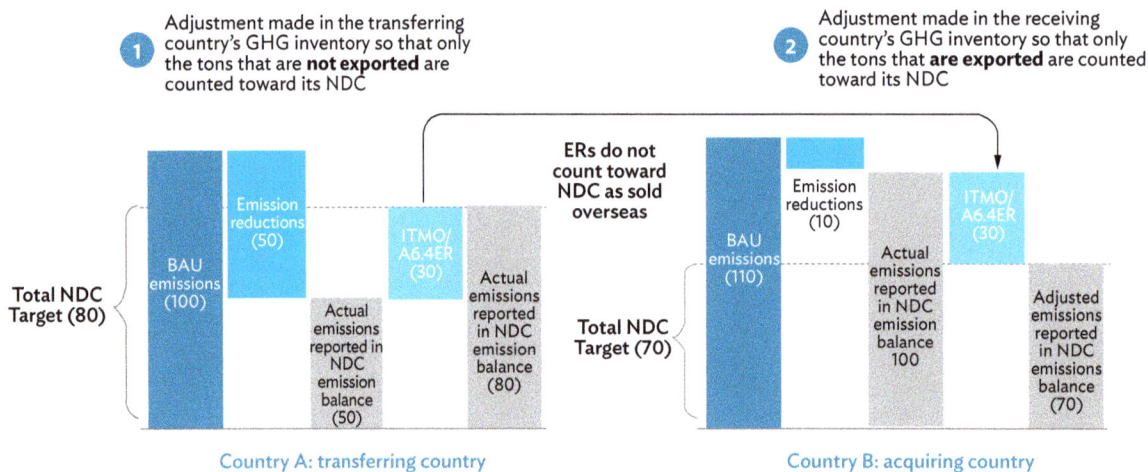

1 Adjustment made in the transferring country's GHG inventory so that only the tons that are **not exported** are counted toward its NDC

2 Adjustment made in the receiving country's GHG inventory so that only the tons that **are exported** are counted toward its NDC

ERs do not count toward NDC as sold overseas

Country A: transferring country

Total NDC Target (80)

BAU emissions (100)

Emission reductions (50)

Actual emissions reported in NDC emission balance (50)

ITMO/A6.4ER (30)

Actual emissions reported in NDC emission balance (80)

Country B: acquiring country

Total NDC Target (70)

BAU emissions (110)

Emission reductions (10)

Actual emissions reported in NDC emission balance 100

ITMO/A6.4ER (30)

Adjusted emissions reported in NDC emissions balance (70)

BAU = business as usual; GHG = greenhouse gas; ITMO = internationally transferred mitigation outcome; NDC = nationally determined contribution.

Source: Figure developed for this report by the Asian Development Bank and Pollination.

Article 6.2

The Article 6.2 guidance affords parties options in the use of high-integrity market approaches to achieve their NDCs and has the potential to increase the global flow of carbon finance. Article 6.2 guidance does not specify the type of activities or how an activity cycle should be designed. The design of the cooperation is left to the participating countries.

However, it also imposes steps and safeguards on carbon transfers, including requirements for authorization, corresponding adjustments, and robust reporting, each of which will be covered in greater detail in the following sections.

While pilot Article 6.2 transfers are under development between several countries and some countries have begun to implement Article 6 governance processes, most countries are preparing the required infrastructure and governance procedures to enable full implementation of Article 6.2 cooperative approaches. Uncertainties remain on how Article 6.2 transactions will be effectuated. Box 2 shares insights from the Joint Crediting Mechanism, a project-based bilateral market-based mechanism initiated by the Government of Japan, which is largely considered a forerunner to Article 6.2 of the Paris Agreement.

Box 2: Joint Crediting Mechanism as the Forerunner to Article 6.2

The Joint Crediting Mechanism (JCM) is a project-based bilateral market-based mechanism initiated in 2013 by the Government of Japan in collaboration with seven partner countries. It is widely viewed as a forerunner for voluntary cooperation using market-based mechanisms under Article 6.2 of the Paris Agreement.[a] The JCM will contribute to the achievement of NDCs of the partner countries and Japan while ensuring the avoidance of double counting through corresponding adjustments. The JCM has already demonstrated how a bilateral cooperative approach can be designed and implemented to not only foster mitigation actions and generate mitigation outcomes but also contribute to achieving the Sustainable Development Goals.

As of June 2023, there were 26 JCM partner countries around the world, including 16 developing member countries of the Asian Development Bank (ADB). Several financing mechanisms facilitate the implementation of the JCM. The Financing Program for JCM Model Projects implemented by the Ministry of the Environment of Japan is one such mechanism, with more than 200 projects selected for financial support. ADB also has a trust fund called the Japan Fund for the Joint Crediting Mechanism, which aims to provide financial incentives for the adoption of advanced low-carbon technologies in ADB-financed and administered sovereign and nonsovereign projects.

After COP26, the JCM partner countries and Japan have been in discussion to incorporate key elements of the guidance on cooperative approaches under Article 6.2 into the rules and guidelines of the JCM, such as (i) arrangements for authorizing the use of JCM credits as internationally transferred mitigation outcomes toward the achievement of NDCs, (ii) application of corresponding adjustments, and (iii) description of how the JCM is consistent with the sustainable development objectives, among others. For the domestic process in Japan to align with the guidance, the Government of Japan established the JCM Promotion and Utilization Council consisting of five ministries, and the council has formalized the procedures for the authorization and corresponding adjustment regarding the JCM.

_____

COP26 = 26th Conference of the Parties of the United Nations Framework Convention on Climate Change.
[a] ADB. 2021. *Article 6 of the Paris Agreement: Drawing Lessons from the Joint Crediting Mechanism* (Version II). Manila.
Source: ADB.

Article 6.4

Article 6.4 establishes a centralized mechanism with a UNFCCC-governed credit issuance body that can facilitate international investment in mitigation activities in exchange for unitized mitigation outcomes while supporting sustainable development. The mechanism is also intended to succeed the CDM but with key differences, for instance, a stronger involvement of the host country. The infrastructure required for full implementation of Article 6.4 was further developed at COP27. With respect to the Article 6.4 registry, the following were agreed upon:

(i) the registry will take the form of a standardized electronic database, which will also make nonconfidential information publicly available through the internet;

(ii) standardization and automatization through the specification of electronic formats; and

(iii) interoperability of registries instituted under Articles 6.4 and 6.2 with each other and any national registries of the parties through provisions developed by the Subsidiary Body for Scientific and Technological Advice.

The new mechanism will ultimately require project or program proponents to register their activity with the Supervisory Body based on approved methodologies. The Supervisory Body develops detailed rules and procedures for approving methodologies, validation, and verification. Countries are also exploring allowable and efficient pathways for transitioning CDM projects historically generating CERs into approved projects that will generate A6.4ERs.[11]

At COP27, parties agreed that the Article 6.4 mechanism registry shall track A6.4ERs that are

(i)   Authorized toward the achievement of an acquiring country's NDC or for other international mitigation purposes—known as Authorized A6.4ERs—which, when authorized for international transfer, are also governed under the Article 6.2 corresponding adjustment and reporting requirements to ensure no double counting; or

(ii)   Not authorized for use toward the achievement of an NDC or other international mitigation purposes, known as Mitigation Contribution A6.4ERs.[12]

Both Authorized A6.4ERs and Mitigation Contribution A6.4ERs will be separately designated in the mechanism registry. Unlike the requirements for international transfers under Article 6.2, the Article 6.4 mechanism requires the application of a share of proceeds whereby 5% of the issued A6.4ERs will be transferred to a registry account held by the Adaptation Fund to help vulnerable countries meet the costs of adaptation, as well as the automatic cancellation of at least 2% of all A6.4ERs to deliver overall mitigation of global emissions.

Other International Mitigation Purposes

Voluntary Carbon Markets

VCMs encompass the collection of standard bodies, voluntary buyers, and carbon credit generators that sell verified carbon credits to be used for voluntary purposes. Carbon crediting programs or standards set the requirements for delivering and measuring emission reductions and removals resulting from a mitigation activity.

The total value of VCMs nearly quadrupled in 2021, reaching almost $2 billion. After several years of rapid growth, the VCM slowed in 2022 with a decline in both the issuance and retirement of carbon credits. Macroeconomic headwinds as well as growing scrutiny on corporate use of carbon credits have contributed to the decline.[13] The market continues to be driven by corporate demand for credits to meet voluntary climate targets (e.g., net zero by 2050), increased interest from investors that see the trade of carbon credits as an investment opportunity, and rising credit prices driving investment into carbon credit supply. While corporate voluntary demand dominates the VCM, the VCM is a fraction of the cap-and-trade compliance market where covered entities are required to surrender allowances for their emissions.

VCMs could support the trade of both authorized and non-authorized mitigation outcomes. Authorized mitigation outcomes have, by definition, been authorized by the host country for international transfer and are subject to a corresponding adjustment in the host country's national accounts. Non-authorized mitigation outcomes have not been authorized by the host country for international transfer and, accordingly, have not been subject to a corresponding adjustment.

---

[11]   CDM project participants must communicate their request to transition activities to the Article 6.4 mechanism by 31 December 2023 to the UNFCCC Secretariat and the host country. The host country must approve the transition by 31 December 2025 at the latest.

[12]   UNFCCC, CMA. 2022. Decision 7/CMA.4, Guidance on the Mechanism Established by Article 6, paragraph 4, of the Paris Agreement. Annex I, para. 29.

[13]   World Bank. 2023. *States and Trends of Carbon Pricing 2023*.

The presence of both authorized and non-authorized mitigation outcomes is likely to create bifurcation in VCMs, whereby authorized mitigation outcomes that have been correspondingly adjusted will be considered more valuable than non-authorized mitigation outcomes.

Some standards are already preparing to trade both authorized and non-authorized carbon credits by introducing labels to tag carbon credits issued within their registry (noting that it is only sovereign governments that may make the authorization and corresponding adjustment). Figure 5 demonstrates how authorized and non-authorized units issued following Articles 6.2 and 6.4 interact with the VCM.

Figure 5: Interplay between Article 6 and the Voluntary Carbon Market

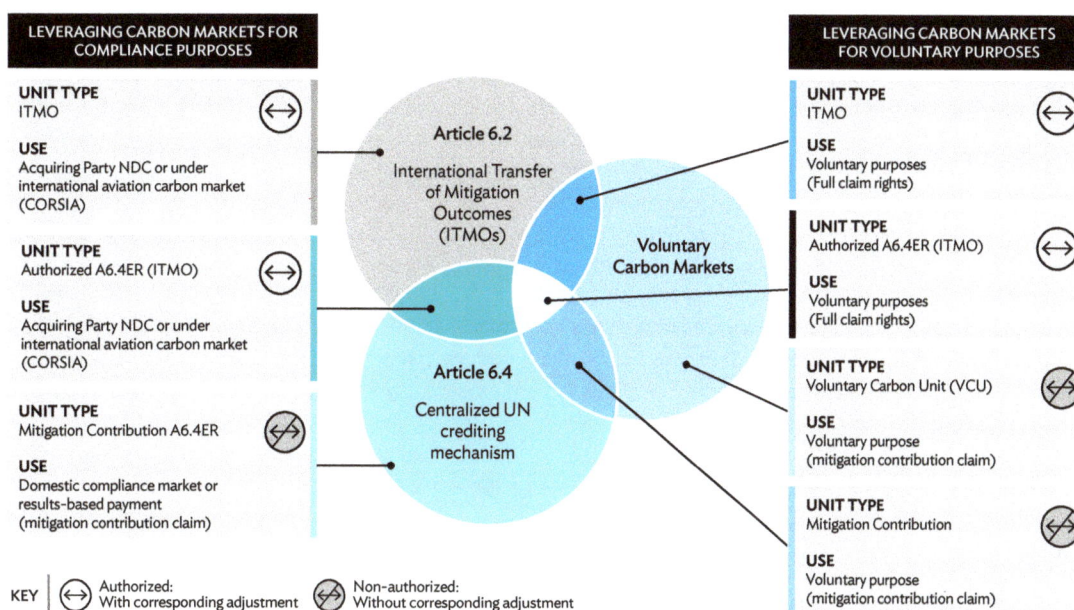

LEVERAGING CARBON MARKETS FOR COMPLIANCE PURPOSES

UNIT TYPE
ITMO

USE
Acquiring Party NDC or under international aviation carbon market (CORSIA)

UNIT TYPE
Authorized A6.4ER (ITMO)

USE
Acquiring Party NDC or under international aviation carbon market (CORSIA)

UNIT TYPE
Mitigation Contribution A6.4ER

USE
Domestic compliance market or results-based payment (mitigation contribution claim)

LEVERAGING CARBON MARKETS FOR VOLUNTARY PURPOSES

UNIT TYPE
ITMO

USE
Voluntary purposes (Full claim rights)

UNIT TYPE
Authorized A6.4ER (ITMO)

USE
Voluntary purposes (Full claim rights)

UNIT TYPE
Voluntary Carbon Unit (VCU)

USE
Voluntary purpose (mitigation contribution claim)

UNIT TYPE
Mitigation Contribution

USE
Voluntary purpose (mitigation contribution claim)

Article 6.2 — International Transfer of Mitigation Outcomes (ITMOs)

Article 6.4 — Centralized UN crediting mechanism

Voluntary Carbon Markets

KEY — Authorized: With corresponding adjustment — Non-authorized: Without corresponding adjustment

A6.4ER = Article 6.4 Emission Reduction Unit, CORSIA = Carbon Offsetting and Reduction Scheme for International Aviation, ITMO = international transfer for mitigation outcomes, NDC = nationally determined contribution, UN = United Nations.
Source: Figure developed for this report by Pollination.

As demand for carbon credits and the overall size of VCMs grows, organizations—including nongovernment organizations, corporates, and governments—are pushing for greater integrity of VCMs in terms of the carbon credits created as well as the claims made by purchasers.

Accurate greenhouse gas (GHG) accounting across the full value chain of carbon credits and avoiding perceptions of misleading claims of how credits are used, will be increasingly important to the integrity of VCMs. This requires ensuring that emission reductions and removals underpinning carbon credits are real, measurable, additional, and permanent, and avoid double counting and leakage. On the supply side, the Integrity Council for the Voluntary Carbon Market (ICVCM) is setting "definitive global threshold standards" that will shift the market toward trading in high-quality carbon credits and efficiently mobilize finance toward urgent mitigation and climate-resilient development. Similarly, on the demand side, the Voluntary Carbon Markets Integrity Initiative (VCMI) is seeking to "drive credible, net-zero aligned participation in voluntary carbon markets" by developing rules to guide corporates in the use of carbon credits to offset emissions and the making of accurate claims regarding their climate benefits. Box 3 provides more information on the ICVCM Core Carbon Principles and the VCMI Claims Code of Practice, including efforts between the organizations to work together to enhance VCM integrity.

Box 3: Efforts for a High Integrity Voluntary Carbon Market

The Integrity Council for the Voluntary Carbon Market (ICVCM) has issued its Core Carbon Principles (CCPs) to enhance supply-side voluntary carbon market (VCM) integrity, while the Voluntary Carbon Markets Integrity Initiative (VCMI) has issued its Claims Code of Practice to enhance demand-side integrity. The CCPs aim to provide "credible, rigorous, and readily accessible" global threshold standards for high-quality or high integrity carbon credits that create real, additional, and verifiable climate impact, in line with the 1.5 Celsius goal of the Paris Agreement, while avoiding negative environmental and social side effects. The CCPs outline guidance for assessing the quality of carbon credits. They seek to create industry-wide guidelines and be compatible with (and promote consistency between) VCM carbon crediting programs and standards such as Verra and Gold Standard. Meanwhile, the Claims Code of Practice aims to provide clear requirements, recommendations, and supporting guidance to companies and other non-state actors in the pursuit of climate targets, and to provide guidance on associated claims they can make regarding the use of carbon credits. The Claims Code of Practice focuses on claims made by carbon market participants by providing three tiers of certification representing varying levels of reliance on carbon credits to meet Paris-aligned climate goals. It is worthwhile noting that the VCMI requires companies to use the highest quality carbon credits, and carbon credit users to publicly report key details, including whether carbon credits used are authorized and correspondingly adjusted following Article 6.

In June 2023, ICVCM and VCMI announced that they would coordinate their efforts to operationalize high-integrity carbon markets and accelerate global climate action. With coordinated launches of the CCPs and Claims Code of Practice in 2023, the two organizations seek to support the private sector when investing in carbon credits as part of efforts to rapidly decarbonize operations and value chains.

Sources: ICVCM. n.d. Core Carbon Principles; and VCMI. 2023. Claims Code of Practice.

One of the dominant considerations related to integrity—particularly concerning the VCMI's work relating to claims guidance—is the approach to addressing double claiming. Double claiming occurs when the same emission reduction or removal is "claimed" by two entities toward achieving climate mitigation targets or goals.

The issue of double claiming becomes more complicated in the context of the Paris Agreement because every country has its climate target, but the Article 6 guidance and rules do not prescribe how countries account for mitigation outcomes claimed by voluntary buyers toward their climate targets. The Article 6 guidance and rules allow for corresponding adjustments to be made for the transfer of mitigation outcomes for "other purposes." This could include the trade of units voluntarily in VCMs if there are buyers that prefer such units, as well as for compliance use under CORSIA.

With the availability of authorized and correspondingly adjusted carbon credits for VCM use, the continued tightening of standards for credit use—and the nature of legitimate carbon claims—the VCM is expected to see an increased demand for authorized credits, at considerably higher prices than non-authorized credit. However, it is too early to make assertions about the future market size of authorized versus unauthorized credits in the VCM and the overall volume of VCM versus the compliance market. The VCM seems to be at a junction where prices are depressed over doubts by buyers over the integrity of credits and buyers understand the importance of high integrity credits and are determining how to assess credit quality and appropriate claims amid ambiguous guidelines.[14] It is also important to note that authorized projects tend to represent higher ambition—to not overlap with the domestic

14   Read more at S. Twidale and S. Mcfarlane. 2023. Carbon credit market confidence ebbs as big names retreat. *Reuters*. 2 September.

NDC implementation—and will be sold at higher costs than unauthorized units under the VCM so although they gain in robustness and legitimacy, there is a cost trade-off. A new balance will emerge as the first countries start authorizing projects for use in the VCM and a Paris-aligned global regime further solidifies.

Carbon Offsetting and Reduction Scheme for International Aviation

Figure 6: Tentative List of Units Eligible under the CORSIA Framework

Certain units under the following emissions reduction programs are eligible under the CORSIA framework

1. American Carbon Registry
2. Architecture for REDD+ Transactions
3. China GHG Voluntary Emission Reduction Program
4. Clean Development Mechanism
5. Climate Action Reserve
6. Forest Carbon Partnership Facility
7. Global Carbon Council
8. Gold Standard
9. Verified Carbon Standard

ELIGIBLE OFFSETS

CORSIA = Carbon Offsetting and Reduction Scheme for International Aviation, GHG = greenhouse gas, REDD+ = Reducing emissions from deforestation and forest degradation, foster conservation, sustainable management of forests and enhancement of forest carbon stock.
Note: Some of the listed schemes are under review and this list is tentative.
Source: Figure developed for this report by Pollination.

In 2010, the International Civil Aviation Organization (ICAO) and its member states agreed to halt aviation emissions at 2020 levels, requiring carbon neutral growth from 2020. The international aviation mitigation measures and rules are outlined through CORSIA, which applies to international aviation emissions only. CORSIA is expected to result in significant demand for international trade in mitigation outcomes, which will fall within the category of "other international mitigation purposes" referred to in the Article 6 guidelines and rules.

As of March 2023, nine offset standards were accepted under CORSIA for the 2021–2023 compliance period; however, some specific methodologies under those programs have been deemed ineligible.[15] For the 2024–2026 compliance period, only units from the American Carbon Registry and Architecture for REDD+ transactions have been accepted under CORSIA.[16] As outlined in Article 6, mitigation outcomes used under CORSIA require authorization from the host government and the application of a corresponding adjustment to avoid double counting with host country NDCs. CORSIA's corresponding adjustment requirement represents a key market signal and source of demand for correspondingly adjusted units. The list of units eligible under the CORSIA framework for 2021–2023 has been visualized in Figure 6, noting that the revised list of CORSIA eligible schemes for the 2024-2026 compliance period and their scope will be published toward the end of 2023, subject to the confirmation of current schemes and new applications.

---

[15] International Civil Aviation Organization (ICAO). n.d. CORDIA Eligible Emissions Units.
[16] ICAO. CORDIA Eligible Emissions Units. p. 9.

Domestic Carbon Pricing Systems

Many jurisdictions have implemented and/or are considering implementing domestic compliance carbon pricing policies. There are two main forms of direct carbon pricing instruments: a carbon tax and an emissions trading system (ETS):

(i)   A carbon tax puts an explicit carbon price on emissions, imposed by the government. Entities are therefore incentivized to reduce their emissions and pay the carbon tax on their remaining emissions.

(ii) An ETS (or domestic carbon market) sets a quantitative limit or cap on emissions and requires participants to "surrender" an allowance for every unit of GHG they emit within a compliance period. Participants are either "allocated" units for free or must purchase them from an auction or the market. By allowing trade, a price for allowances emerges based on the lowest cost of abatement, which varies with supply of and demand for allowances.

In practice, many jurisdictions implement some combination of both systems, such as an ETS with price floors or both carbon taxes and ETSs with different specifications in the same jurisdictions. Further, some jurisdictions allow covered entities to fulfill part of their carbon tax or ETS obligations through the purchase of domestic or international carbon credits. Such domestic credits can come from domestic crediting mechanisms—such as the South Africa crediting mechanism—or independent crediting schemes.

Depending on system design, domestic carbon pricing systems can interact with the international carbon market in various ways. For example, strong incentives to generate carbon credits for use in a domestic carbon market system may reduce the relative incentives to develop mitigation projects for utilization under either Article 6 or in VCMs generally. This will particularly be the case where the domestic carbon price mechanism supports a higher price than that available on the international carbon market. Alternatively, domestic carbon pricing systems may also allow international credits to be surrendered for compliance.

Article 6.4 will create an international carbon credit mechanism that could be used for compliance through international mitigation outcomes and thus create indirect links across domestic carbon pricing instruments.[17] To balance the benefits and risks of linking with the international market, domestic carbon pricing instruments can adopt qualitative and quantitative restrictions on credit use. Such restrictions are common across carbon pricing instruments.

Carbon Pricing Experience in Asia and the Pacific

An increasing number of countries in Asia and the Pacific have adopted domestic carbon pricing instruments (either a carbon tax or an ETS) in recent years.[18] As of 2023, there are seven carbon pricing systems in Asia and the Pacific at the national level, including two carbon taxes and five ETSs. Countries such as Malaysia, Pakistan, Thailand, and Viet Nam are considering the implementation of a direct carbon price instrument.

---

[17]   If domestic pricing schemes are to contribute to the achievement of the NDCs when including flexibility through international offsets, exports, and imports of mitigation, outcomes from the sectors covered by a scheme should include corresponding adjustments. In this sense, it is the accounting framework under Article 6.2 that creates the indirect bilateral linking of domestic carbon pricing instruments.

[18]   Here, domestic carbon pricing policies are limited to carbon taxes and ETSs.

Examples of domestic pricing systems in the region include:[19]

(i) **Indonesia** has launched a mandatory, intensity-based ETS for the electricity generation sector to commence in 2023. This ETS is intended to eventually operate alongside a carbon tax. Indonesia initially intended the carbon tax element to be introduced in April 2022, but it has been delayed to 2025. It is not clear yet how the carbon tax and ETS are intended to interact. Indonesia has also issued regulations to govern the trading of carbon credits generated in Indonesia into international markets.

(ii) **Japan** has a carbon tax on emissions from the combustion of fossil fuels, with some exceptions for particular sectors. The cities of Tokyo and Saitama have both implemented emissions trading as an approach to limit emissions from their building sectors.

(iii) **Kazakhstan** launched its ETS in January 2013 and by 2020, the system covered about 50% of the country's GHG emissions.

(iv) **New Zealand** has an ETS covering electricity generation, industry, waste, and transport, with the highest carbon price in Asia and the Pacific as of 2023.

(v) The **People's Republic of China (PRC)** has implemented an ETS that applies (as of 2023) to electricity generation and is the largest carbon pricing scheme in Asia and the Pacific (and the world) as of 2023. It also plans to cover industrial emissions in the future but has not published a timeline. Before the launch of the national ETS, the PRC gained valuable experience with emissions trading through the implementation of seven subnational pilot systems.[20]

(vi) The **Republic of Korea**'s ETS was the first national mandatory ETS system in East Asia. It covers electricity generation, industry, buildings, waste, and domestic aviation. The Republic of Korea's ETS also allows limited use of domestic carbon credits external to its ETS as well as international CDM CERs developed by companies in the Republic of Korea.

(vii) **Singapore** has introduced a carbon tax on emissions from all sectors for entities above a certain emissions threshold. As part of its carbon tax revision, the Government of Singapore will allow entities to offset a proportion of their carbon tax obligations (5%) through the purchase of high-quality international carbon credits subject to Article 6.2 guidance.

In addition to these countries, there are different types of domestic carbon pricing systems—albeit those that price carbon indirectly—in Asia and the Pacific including crediting mechanisms such as the Thailand Voluntary Emission Reduction Scheme (T-VER) and schemes such as the Perform, Achieve and Trade (PAT) in India. In addition, the Government of India has taken steps toward the implementation of a carbon market. As outlined by the Bureau of Energy Efficiency in a draft blueprint, India is proposing a phased introduction of a voluntary market followed by a compliance market with mandatory participation for covered entities.

Some national and subnational governments outside Asia and the Pacific have "linked" their domestic carbon pricing schemes, allowing for carbon credits or allowances to be transferred across borders in service of meeting their compliance obligations.[21]

---

[19] The following summaries are based on those provided by the International Carbon Action Partnership; World Bank States and Trends Report 2023. International Carbon Action Partnership. 2023. Offset Use Across Emissions Trading Systems. January.

[20] Beijing, Chongqing, Guangdong, Hubei, Shanghai, Shenzhen, and Tianjin.

[21] For example, California in the United States and Quebec in Canada.

Legal and Policy Frameworks to Operationalize International Carbon Markets through Article 6

3

As international carbon markets are an evolving space—with activity intensifying following the resolution of the Article 6 guidance and rules at COP26 in 2021—many jurisdictions lack these requisite frameworks, and some require capability and resourcing requirements to develop them.

While some technical elements of the Article 6 guidance and rules remain under negotiation, there is already enough direction for countries to develop the national frameworks necessary to participate in Article 6. To participate in cooperative approaches under Article 6 and leverage the opportunities for external financing that they present, countries will need to ensure that the appropriate legal, policy, and institutional frameworks are in place at the national level.

This chapter highlights the pathways for engagement with international carbon markets by shedding insights on key issues to be considered in establishing core legal and policy frameworks that will be required to operationalize Article 6 at the national level and the key considerations on which countries will need to reach a position when determining their approach.

Summary: Core Strategy and National Frameworks for Article 6 Operationalization

There are several legal, regulatory, and institutional frameworks that countries will need to establish to operationalize Article 6 transparently and effectively.

The core frameworks required include the following:

(i) **Strategy for the achievement of the nationally determined contributions and Article 6 policy.** Country engagement with Article 6 must be informed by long-term planning for the achievement of their NDCs, including the ratcheting of ambition. This will be important to inform the suitability of mitigation outcomes for international transfer.

(ii) **Legal and policy frameworks to define eligibility**, manage the activity cycle, track mitigation outcomes, and authorize international transfer under Article 6. To engage with Article 6 effectively, host countries will require legal and policy frameworks to support the creation, verification, and accounting of mitigation outcomes—including A6.4 ERs—and effectuate their transfer.[22] Legal and regulatory frameworks must provide clarity on approvals under Article 6 processes, the formal "authorization" of ITMOs for use and transfer, and the legal title associated with mitigation outcomes transferred through those processes.

---

[22] Note that the creation, verification, and accounting of A6.4ERs are governed by the Supervisory Body. Countries may still create supporting legal and policy frameworks that create an enabling environment for these projects and enforce national provisions, such as benefit-sharing.

(iii)   **Accounting-and-reporting infrastructure that accommodates Article 6 operationalization.**
Article 6 transactions must be reflected in country NDC tracking and accounting infrastructure through corresponding adjustments implemented following the Article 6 guidance and rules. Countries will also need to be positioned to comply with the reporting requirements specific to Article 6.

The implementation of these frameworks will require collaboration across ministries to ensure alignment. Effective implementation may also require the development of technical and/or regulatory capacity, as well as awareness-building and education in the private sector.

Strategy for Achieving the Nationally Determined Contribution

Countries will need to make a set of strategic decisions regarding the nature of their participation, if any, in the international cooperation established by Article 6. Country strategies should inform these decisions to achieve their NDCs. Ideally, the policy implications of these strategic decisions regarding Article 6 participation will be articulated in a publicly available Article 6 policy. This policy should clearly articulate the country's position on Article 6 transactions including processes for authorization, who is allowed to participate in Article 6 transactions and under what conditions, and the procedures (including payment of taxes or fees if relevant) for participation.

Countries have several avenues through which they could engage in carbon markets to support mitigation activities for NDC achievement and/or beyond NDC mitigation. The following table provides an overview of these strategic approaches along with the advantages and disadvantages associated with them.

Table: Strategic Approaches for Leveraging Carbon Markets

	Leveraging markets for NDC achievement		Leveraging markets for beyond-NDC mitigation	
	Domestic Carbon Pricing	Non-authorized units used for voluntary purposes (VCM)*	International carbon trading under Article 6	Authorized units used for voluntary purposes (VCM)ª
Benefits	• Economic efficiency • Public revenue	• Private investment for NDC achievement	• Diplomatic cooperation • Additional demand (e.g., CORSIA)	• Additional demand (e.g., voluntary buyers seeking units with a corresponding adjustment)
Challenges	• Complex and time consuming to set up • Higher costs for businesses and consumers	• Uncertainty of demand	• Administrative burden	• Administrative burden

CORSIA = Carbon Offsetting and Reduction Scheme for International Aviation, NDC = nationally determined contribution, VCM = voluntary carbon market.
Source: Table developed for this report by the Asian Development Bank and Pollination.

The left side of the table compares the pros and cons of a country leveraging carbon markets for NDC achievement, specifically comparing domestic carbon pricing and non-authorization of mitigation outcomes for voluntary purposes. The right side of the table focuses on options and implications for leveraging carbon markets for mitigation that goes beyond their NDC, i.e., market approaches where mitigation outcomes are correspondingly adjusted from the NDC, which are best considered by countries in the context of attracting finance for mitigation in addition to the NDC target.

These strategic approaches and the available mechanisms that sit within them are not mutually exclusive and may synergize, even within a sector. For example, a country may choose to implement domestic carbon pricing policies for certain sectors or activities to support the NDC achievement, while also undertaking international cooperation in other sectors through Article 6 by transferring mitigation outcomes beyond what is needed to meet the NDC targets. Such approaches are under discussion in Indonesia.

In either case, countries should establish the national arrangements and the legal architecture to support carbon credit authorization, even if there is no decision to use markets for beyond-NDC mitigation. The demand and price for non-authorized and authorized credits may change, as is the nature of demand-driven markets. As a country may want to adapt its strategy, establishing a regulatory framework that will support future participation in cooperative approaches under Article 6 is prudent.

Countries may also consider linking their domestic carbon pricing instruments to international carbon markets. For example, Singapore allows companies to use correspondingly adjusted international carbon credits to pay for a portion of their domestic carbon tax liability.[23]

Another consideration for countries as they develop a strategy for the achievement of their NDC and determine their approach to engaging with international carbon markets, is to take stock of their previous experience with international carbon markets, such as the CDM of the Kyoto Protocol. The Article 6 Rules guide the activities and credits that can be transitioned from the CDM to the Article 6.4 mechanism of the Paris Agreement (Box 4). In addition, countries have a host of experience, as well as human and technical capacity from the CDM that can be useful while setting the institutions and frameworks to operationalize Article 6 of the Paris Agreement.

Three additional things are particularly important to consider when developing a strategy for NDC achievement: clarity on carbon and climate finance; implications of corresponding adjustments for national climate objectives; and treatment of VCMs in the context of Article 6.

Box 4: Considerations for Transitioning Activities from the Clean Development Mechanism

As part of a broader Article 6 engagement strategy, countries may wish to leverage their portfolio of CDM projects to jumpstart their engagement in Article 6. Under the Article 6.4 rules, modalities, and procedures, eligible CDM projects may transition to the Article 6.4 mechanism provided they meet the Article 6.4 requirements and have host country approval.[a] Proponents of CDM projects in transitioning to the Article 6.4 mechanism must communicate their request to transition to the UNFCCC Secretariat and the host country no later than 31 December 2023, and host countries have until 31 December 2025 to consider and approve these requests. CDM projects for transition may continue to use CDM methodologies until 31 December 2025, or until the end of the current crediting period, whichever comes first.[b] From 2026, transitioned projects must utilize Article 6.4 methodologies and fulfill all Article 6.4 requirements. Article 6.4. The Supervisory Body is developing and/or approving methodologies, which is a key element that must be in place to facilitate the CDM project transition.

At COP26, countries agreed that CERs under the CDM may be counted toward NDC achievement during the first NDC period only, provided the project was registered on or after 1 January 2013.[c] CERs can be internationally transferred and used by an acquiring country toward its NDC; however, transferred CERs are not considered ITMOs, as ITMOs, by definition, are generated from 2021 onward, whereas CERs are pre-2021.

continued on next page

---

23   IETA. 2022. Carbon Market Business Brief: Singapore. June.

Box 4 *continued*

Transfer of CERs for the use of the first NDCs will need to be carefully considered and may not be the best cause of action for all countries. The Asian Development Bank published a report with an in-depth discussion of the transfer of CERs.[d]

CDM = Clean Development Mechanism, CER = certified emission reduction, COP26 = 26th Conference of the Parties, ITMO = internationally transferred mitigation outcome, NDC = nationally determined contribution, UNFCCC = United Nations Framework Convention on Climate Change.

[a] UNFCCC, Conference of the Parties serving as the meeting of the Parties to the Paris Agreement (CMA). 2021. Decision 3/CMA.3, Rules, Modalities and Procedures for the Mechanism established by Article 6, paragraph 4, of the Paris Agreement, Annex, para. 73; and UNFCCC, CMA. 2022. Decision 7/CMA.4, Guidance on the Mechanism Established by Article 6, paragraph 4, of the Paris Agreement. Annex, Chapter I.

[b] UNFCCC, CMA. 2021. Decision 3/CMA.3, Rules, Modalities and Procedures for the Mechanism Established by Article 6, paragraph 4, of the Paris Agreement, Annex, para. 73.

[c] UNFCCC, CMA. 2021. Decision 3/CMA.3, Rules, Modalities and Procedures for the Mechanism Established by Article 6, paragraph 4, of the Paris Agreement, Annex, para. 75.

[d] Asian Development Bank. 2021. *From Kyoto to Paris—Transitioning the Clean Development Mechanism*. Manila.

Source: Asian Development Bank.

Clarity on Carbon and Climate Finance

Various forms of finance are available to countries to support NDC implementation, and in planning finance needs for NDC achievement, countries should consider the costs and benefits of accessing the broad range of finance that is available for countries including both climate finance that do not involve the use of carbon markets as well as carbon finance.

Generally, "carbon finance" refers to finance mobilized from the use of carbon market based measures including participation in carbon markets without applying corresponding adjustments (e.g., VCM activity without corresponding adjustments or domestic carbon pricing policies). While carbon finance is inherently results-based finance, carbon markets can also be utilized to mobilize finance in instances where emission units are generated, but they are canceled without any party claiming or counting it as part of their climate ambition. This is classified differently than "other climate finance" which generally refers to public finance delivered toward the $100 billion finance goal and under Article 9 of the Paris Agreement.

Countries can utilize both sources of finance to achieve an NDC. Generally, action with domestic means and climate finance can be used to achieve the pledged unconditional NDC targets. These are usually low-hanging fruits, in that they can be achieved without additional international support. Meanwhile, carbon markets can be used for sectors that are under the conditional NDC or perhaps even not mentioned in the NDC, which would be high-hanging fruits that are desired by the host country but not achievable with the means available. Delivering on such sectors may require additional international support through, for example, technology transfer or capacity building. To this end, those measures contribute to innovation, improved livelihood, investment, and job creation, while not limiting the ability of the country to achieve its pledged target. Additionally, mitigation actions that are more costly to deliver may be remunerated with a higher price, as should mitigation outcomes that deliver associated environment and/or social co-benefits for which a buyer may pay a premium.

Implications of Corresponding Adjustments for National Climate Objectives

The international cooperation facilitated by Article 6 is intended to enable parties to raise their ambition under the Paris Agreement. However, countries may "over-export" ITMOs, which could result in the country failing to meet its NDC target or disincentivizing it from increasing its NDC ambition. Any country that allows ITMO exports and subsequently fails to meet its NDC risks criticism that it over-exported ITMOs, irrespective of whether the reason for failing to meet its NDC bears any relation to the transfer of ITMOs. While failing to meet NDC targets could be viewed as a separate matter beyond the scope of Article 6 transfers (provided corresponding adjustments are properly applied), NDC underachievement by parties exporting ITMOs may negatively impact the future use of Article 6 as a tool for enhancing ambition. While the exporting party largely bears this risk, there could potentially be buyer-side risks that may concern both sovereigns and authorized private parties transacting in ITMOs.[24]

Overselling can be a result of[25]

(i)   Selling low-cost mitigation outcomes that are necessary for meeting the NDC target;

(ii)   Selling mitigation outcomes that do not represent reductions;

(iii) Selling mitigation outcomes for which the reduction in emissions will not be captured by the transferring country's GHG inventory; or

(iv)   Selling mitigation outcomes generated outside the scope of the NDC, since guidance requires corresponding adjustments for these transfers.

The host country can adopt several strategies to avoid overselling. These can be categorized into four broad groups of strategies:

(i)   Ensuring that mitigation outcomes that the country intends to use to achieve its NDC are not authorized for international transfer under Article 6.

(ii)   Not transferring all the mitigation outcomes that are generated from cooperative mitigation actions.

(iii) Implementing pricing strategies that create a pool of funds, potentially generated from the sale and transfer of ITMOs, to invest in additional mitigation if necessary to achieve its NDC.

(iv)   Using conservative baselines to reduce the risk of overstating mitigation outcomes.

To avoid a scenario where a country over-exports ITMOs, the host country should undertake a detailed assessment of its NDC targets and its implementation plan to estimate the likely mitigation outcomes of those efforts (NDC implementation plan) to project whether the host country is on a trajectory to meet and exceed its NDC targets (taking into consideration both conditional and unconditional elements of these targets). Establishing appropriate accounting and reporting infrastructure for mitigation outcomes and ITMOs will be important for countries to be able to track progress in achieving their NDCs and avoid overselling.

In addition to host country strategies, prudent countries purchasing ITMOs can also observe the ability of host countries to meet their NDC while participating in cooperative approaches under Article 6, particularly under Article 6.2. For example, Switzerland will discontinue cooperation with a country if it becomes evident that the country will not reach the NDC targets.

---

24   For further reading on buy-side risk considerations, please see Pollination. 2021. Legal Gap Analysis for Transactions in Preparation for Article 6. May.

25   R. Spalding-Fecher et al. 2020. Practical strategies to avoid over-selling. Oslo, Norway: Carbon Limits.

Article 6 guidance does not prevent countries with NDC targets defined in non-GHG metrics from participating in cooperative approaches. However, if the cooperative approach is implemented using non-GHG metrics, the country will need to quantify any non-GHG metrics used in the NDC into GHG metrics, following the guidance for Article 6.2.[26]

Treatment of Voluntary Carbon Markets in the Context of Article 6

Finance raised through participation in VCMs can be considered a form of carbon finance to be evaluated by host governments in designing their approach to carbon markets. Typically, countries have not regulated VCMs; however, they exist in the context of national legal and regulatory frameworks and governments have various legal, policy, and regulatory "levers" they can pull to influence their country's interaction with VCMs. A key prerequisite for countries to harness VCMs to support their NDC goals is to have visibility over VCM activity involving domestic mitigation projects and be able to track and trace the associated emissions reductions and removals.

Article 6 guidance does not apply to the use of non-authorized carbon credits by voluntary buyers in the VCM. However, countries can benefit from developing policy positions regarding the role of VCMs in meeting its NDC, i.e., whether it will authorize (and consequently correspondingly adjust) credits for use toward a voluntary target, or whether it will not authorize the export of those credits and will count the GHG reductions or removals underpinning those credits toward its NDC. In the absence of corresponding adjustments, the buyer would be sharing the claim of emission reductions or removals with the host country so it would not have an exclusive right to the claim. A country's decision on which mitigation outcomes to authorize for use in VCMs will need to be informed by analysis regarding the NDC trajectory, costs of implementation, and which sources of finance are most appropriate to meet those costs. Countries will also need to consider buyer perspectives and the size of the demand for authorized versus non-authorized units. Countries could make this policy decision on a case-by-case basis for each carbon financing opportunity or provide blanket policy positioning applicable to all VCM activities.

The decision on Article 6.4 at COP27 introduces a unit (mitigation contribution A.64ERs) for the cases where no authorization is done.[27] The unit can be used for results-based climate finance, domestic mitigation pricing schemes, or domestic price-based measures, to contribute to the reduction of emission levels in the host party. Figure 7 shows the implications of using non-authorized versus authorized mitigation outcomes for voluntary purposes.

---

[26]   UNFCCC, CMA. 2021. Decision 2/CMA.3, Guidance on Cooperative Approaches Referred to in Article 6, paragraph 2, of the Paris Agreement. Annex, para. 22(d).

[27]   UNFCCC, CMA. 2022. Decision /CMA.4 Guidance on the mechanism established by Article 6, paragraph 4, of the Paris Agreement. Annex. para. 29(b).

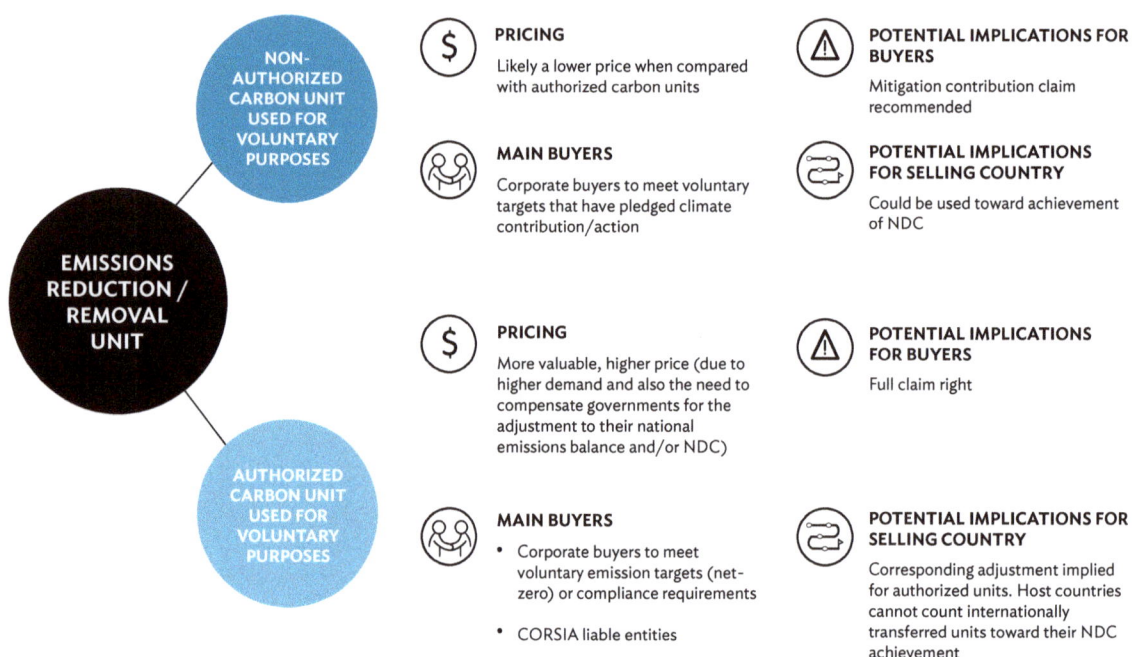

Figure 7: Implications of Using Non-authorized versus Authorized Mitigation Outcomes for Voluntary Purposes

CORSIA = Carbon Offsetting and Reduction Scheme for International Aviation, NDC = nationally determined contribution.
Source: Figure developed for this report by the Asian Development Bank and Pollination.

Governance Structures to Support the Development and Implementation of Article 6 Policies

Countries will require a governance structure to support the development and implementation of their Article 6 policy, including assigning roles and oversight for key operational functions, monitoring and evaluation, and iteration.

These governance bodies are particularly important where legal frameworks for carbon market engagement and Article 6 are absent or under development, as they can play a role in guiding the development of these legal frameworks, including processes for making decisions regarding carbon market engagement and negotiating bilateral agreements. These governance bodies may be formally established under legislation or using other administrative powers of government departments.

Countries need to establish a cross-ministerial decision group that can reconcile, to the extent required, different ministry perspectives and priorities in achieving the NDC.

Further, the countries should seek endorsement for the Article 6 policy from core stakeholders—including the private sector, environmental groups, and civil society—to ensure there is alignment and support from all levels of government and various ministries, as well as the broader community.

Clarity in the Legal Nature of Carbon Credits

Carbon credits represent a relatively novel legal concept. Globally there are a range of legal forms that carbon credits have taken. These include forms of intangible property, personal property, financial instruments, or simply contractual rights.[28] The legal nature of carbon credits influences rights to generate, own, and use carbon credits, and the way that they are accounted for, regulated, and taxed.[29] As such, clarity in the legal nature of carbon credits is required to support market participation.

Clarity in Rights to Generate, Own, and Use Carbon Credits, Including Property Rights and Land-Tenure Considerations Relevant to Mitigation Activities

Clarity in the allocation of rights to generate, own, and use mitigation outcomes is vital for carbon markets to function effectively, and core to carbon credit purchaser due diligence (footnote 29). The inability to establish the proper carbon rights holder may hamper a seller's ability to transfer unencumbered carbon credits, which impacts the perceived integrity of the credit and ultimately its value in the market. Accordingly, countries that fail to provide clarity in the allocation of these rights may compromise private sector investment opportunities.[30]

In particular, host countries must have legal frameworks in place to provide clarity on property rights and land tenure for mitigation activities; legal ownership of mitigation activities; whether title is transferable; the ownership of land where mitigation activities are located (including areas where property rights are typically more complex, such as the coastal zone); and customary land rights and controls, if any, over foreign ownership of land.

The property rights and tenure requirements relevant to mitigation activities and resulting carbon assets differ between jurisdictions. In some countries, underlying rights to emissions reductions and removals are owned by the government, allowing it substantial control over the sale and use of carbon credits generated through carbon mitigation activities. For instance, Peru has taken a centralized approach to carbon rights, with the Payment for Ecosystem Services Law, Law No. 30215 declaring that carbon sequestration and storage—including from REDD+ activities—is the "patrimony of the nation."[31] Entities that achieve these ecosystem services are, however, entitled to receive compensation for doing so, provided they seek approval from the Government of Peru, and the governance and financial arrangements are documented in a central registry. In other countries such as Australia, legal and regulatory frameworks—specifically state-based property laws—provide private landholders with full rights to carbon credits generated on their land, and the ability to protect these rights by registering the rights on the property title.

---

[28]   Gold Standard Foundation and EY Law. 2022. Carbon Credit Rights Under the Paris Agreement. For example, carbon credits generated under several independent standards represent private, tradeable certificates that ensure a given activity has met certain criteria and reduced or sequestered a defined quantity of carbon emissions. The legal nature of such carbon credits is an enforceable contractual obligation between two private parties.

[29]   Gold Standard Foundation and EY Law. 2022. Carbon Credit Rights Under the Paris Agreement.

[30]   Carbon asset issuing bodies take differing approaches to proving legal title to carbon credits, which can create ambiguity and disputes over ownership and use of the carbon credits.

[31]   Grantham Research Institute on Climate Change and the Environment. 2014. Mechanisms of Compensation for Services to Ecosystems. Law No. 30215.

Rights Related to Eligible Interest Holders

Countries must ensure that the rights of eligible interest holders are safeguarded under any market-based measures operating in their jurisdiction. This includes grievance mechanisms in place to support stakeholders to protect their rights. This must also include ensuring the rights and knowledge of indigenous peoples and local communities are protected, and that the principle of free, prior, and informed consent (FPIC) is adhered to. The principle of FPIC is enshrined in international conventions: the *United Nations Declaration on the Rights of Indigenous Peoples, the Convention on Biological Diversity*, and the International Labour Organization's Indigenous and Tribal Peoples Convention, 1989 (No. 169).[32]

While the Cancun Safeguards only apply to REDD+ programs, they can help to inform best practice approaches.[33] Countries could also have reference to industry codes such as the Australian Carbon Market Institute's *Australian Carbon Industry Code of Conduct*, which contains specific advice on establishing project ownership and engaging with interest holders.[34] The Australian Indigenous Carbon Industry Network has published a best-practice guide for carbon project developers, *Seeking Free, Prior, and Informed Consent from Indigenous Communities for Carbon Projects*, which may also usefully inform the approach countries take to standard setting for mitigation activities occurring in its jurisdiction.[35] The approach taken in voluntary carbon credit verification standards such as the Climate, Community and Biodiversity Standards—which require projects to meet a range of participation criteria, including obtaining FPIC—may also be useful in this regard.[36]

Benefit-sharing measures are also important to ensure that the advantages and financial benefits derived from mitigation activities are shared equitably with stakeholders. While benefit-sharing arrangements are primarily set at the project level—in line with stakeholder expectations and the requirements of carbon and co-benefit verification standards—jurisdictions can also play a role in mandating minimum benefit-sharing requirements for projects occurring in their jurisdiction.

Foreign Direct Investment through Carbon Finance

There is a range of matters regarding foreign direct investment through carbon finance that will need to be considered and managed by countries, striking a balance between appropriate controls, incentivizing investment in activities aligned with government priorities, and not unduly hindering foreign investment (while also managing national security considerations). These considerations include

(i)   whether government approval for foreign investment in mitigation activities will be required and whether there will be any restrictions on foreign ownership of assets, such as land involved in mitigation activities;

(ii)   whether the country will seek to impose a levy or share of proceeds regime on foreign investment;

(iii) whether the country will restrict the repatriation of profits through foreign exchange controls; and

(iv)   whether the country will have strategies for the use of revenues or proceeds.

---

[32]   United Nations. 2008. United Nations Declaration on the Rights of Indigenous Peoples; United Nations. 1992. *Convention on Biological Diversity*, Article 8(j); International Labour Organization (ILO). 1989. Indigenous and Tribal Peoples Convention (No. 169).

[33]   UNFCCC, Conference of the Parties (COP). 2011. Decision 1/CP.16, The Cancun Agreements: Outcome of the work of the Ad Hoc Working Group on Long-term Cooperative Action under the Convention. Appendix I.

[34]   Australian Carbon Industry. 2021. *Code of Conduct* (Version 2.0).

[35]   Indigenous Carbon Industry Network (ICIN). 2020. Seeking free, prior and informed consent from Indigenous communities for carbon projects: A best guide for carbon project developers.

[36]   Verra. 2022. The CCB Program.

An important thing to consider is the use of additional revenue generated from engagement in carbon markets. Countries can agree to use part of the financing through other mitigation and adaptation strategies in the country beyond those involved in the transfer. This can be achieved by applying a share of proceeds on ITMOs to be used by the transferring country government for financing other mitigation or adaptation measures. In the case of Article 6.4, the contribution of resources by participating parties to the Adaptation Fund is mandatory. Multiple countries are considering agreeing to a share of proceeds in cooperative approaches under Article 6.2 (footnote 9).

Appropriate Fees and/or Levies on the International Transfer of Mitigation Outcomes

Countries will need to determine whether they intend to tax transactions dealing with the international transfer of mitigation outcomes. Doing so could form part of a country's approach to ensuring carbon finance is raised by the government through Article 6 participation either through reinvesting of a share of proceed revenues into climate action, or investment of carbon revenues from projects.

This could take several forms, including retaining a proportion of carbon credits issued, taxing revenues associated with the sale of carbon credits, or charging for the authorization of mitigation outcomes for international transfer. These policy settings could be deployed to gear investment toward certain mitigation opportunities aligned with government priorities. In determining their approach, countries should consider how taxation of transactions will affect domestic market players and their ability to export mitigation outcomes (i.e., the competitiveness of their credits in the international market) and, if taxation is to occur, how the resulting revenues will be used.

Under Ghana's Article 6 framework, administration fees vary according to the category of mitigation activity, with forest activities subject to lower fees than large-scale non-forestry projects. By comparison, Tanzania's administrative fee structure for Article 6 authorizations does not differentiate by sector, but rather by the citizenship status of the requesting individual, with a higher application fee being charged to non-citizen applicants.

Meeting Prerequisites for International Cooperation under Articles 6.2 and 6.4

There are a further set of legal and institutional requirements countries will need to put in place to operationalize Article 6.2 and Article 6.4 in compliance with the Paris Agreement, including the following:

(i) **Mechanisms to track and record mitigation outcomes achieved.** Countries will need to develop accounting frameworks and registries (or have access to an international registry) to measure and track mitigation outcomes achieved within their jurisdiction, as part of the system for tracking progress toward the achievement of the country's NDC;[37] and

---

[37] The establishment of mechanisms to track and record mitigation outcomes achieved is a key practical measure to allow a country to enforce legal and regulatory frameworks for carbon markets and avoid double counting. Countries could enforce the use of these tracking mechanisms by using fines for noncompliance.

(ii) **Authorization procedures aligned with the Article 6 guidance and rules.** For countries to participate in the international transfer of mitigation outcomes under Article 6.2, procedures to govern authorization, including the competent decision-making body, must be established.

Figure 8 summarizes these legal and institutional requirements and their respective sub-elements.

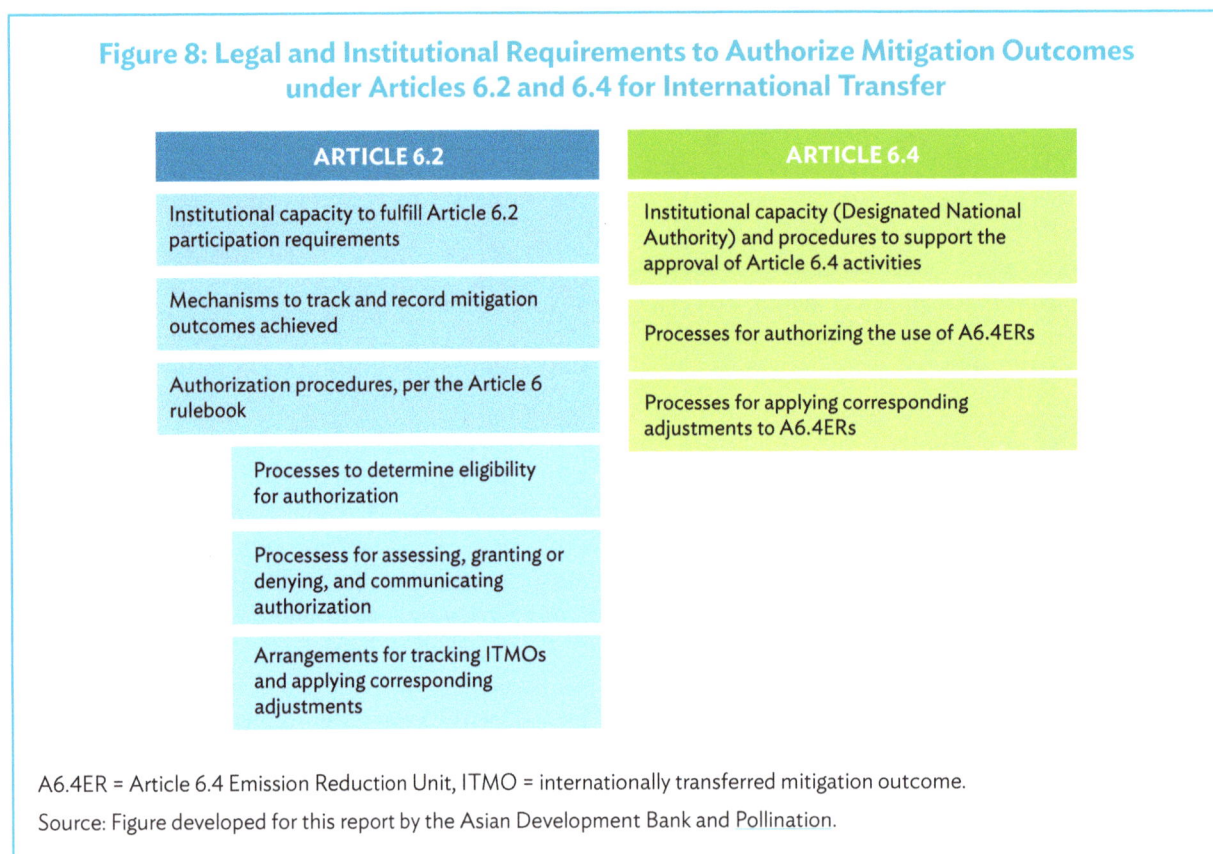

Figure 8: Legal and Institutional Requirements to Authorize Mitigation Outcomes under Articles 6.2 and 6.4 for International Transfer

ARTICLE 6.2	ARTICLE 6.4
Institutional capacity to fulfill Article 6.2 participation requirements	Institutional capacity (Designated National Authority) and procedures to support the approval of Article 6.4 activities
Mechanisms to track and record mitigation outcomes achieved	Processes for authorizing the use of A6.4ERs
Authorization procedures, per the Article 6 rulebook	Processes for applying corresponding adjustments to A6.4ERs
Processes to determine eligibility for authorization	
Processess for assessing, granting or denying, and communicating authorization	
Arrangements for tracking ITMOs and applying corresponding adjustments	

A6.4ER = Article 6.4 Emission Reduction Unit, ITMO = internationally transferred mitigation outcome.

Source: Figure developed for this report by the Asian Development Bank and Pollination.

Accounting and Reporting Infrastructure to Support Article 6 Operationalization

Alongside the legal and institutional requirements to track and authorize mitigation outcomes under Article 6.2 and Article 6.4 for international transfer, the Article 6 guidance and rules envisage several components of accounting and reporting infrastructure to support the operationalization of Article 6.2 and the Article 6.4 mechanism. Parties are responsible for reporting registry information to the Article 6 database, regardless of having a national registry or accounts in the international registry. Information exchange between party registries (whether in the national or international registry) and the Article 6.4 mechanism registry should be made possible. Figure 9 visualizes Article 6 accounting and reporting infrastructure.

Figure 9: Article 6 Accounting and Reporting Infrastructure

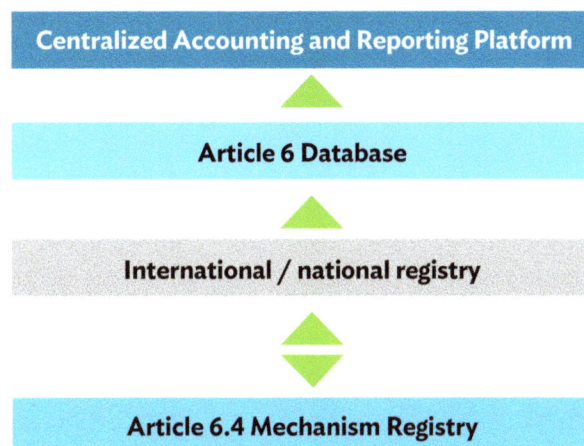

Source: Figure developed for this report by the Asian Development Bank and Pollination.

National Operationalization of Article 6: Lessons from Ghana

In 2022, Ghana adopted its *Framework on International Carbon Markets and Non-Market Approaches,* which is one of the first national Article 6 frameworks developed globally.[38] This detailed framework guides domestic and international actors interested in investing in the generation and/or international transfer of mitigation outcomes in Ghana. In addition to the technical and operational requirements, the framework provides the sample letters, templates, and forms necessary to operationalize the policy. Box 5 captures some of the strategic decisions taken by Ghana for operationalizing Article 6 and the key insights or lessons from this experience for countries.

Box 5: National Operationalization of Article 6—Lessons from Ghana

▶ PROCESSES TO DETERMINE ELIGIBILITY FOR AUTHORIZATION
(INFORMED BY LONG-TERM STRATEGY TO ACHIEVE THE NATIONALLY DETERMINED CONTRIBUTION [NDC])

Ghana Experience

In its national Article 6 framework, Ghana clarifies that it will authorize mitigation outcomes associated with its conditional NDC activities and activities outside the NDC. To clarify which activities fall under the conditional portion of its NDC and are eligible for international transfer, Ghana established a "whitelist" of 25 activity types that form the conditional NDC, including forest conservation activities.

Voluntary carbon market (VCM) projects aiming to generate carbon credits must obtain formal recognition to ensure enhanced accounting in reporting. As explicitly addressed in the framework, VCM projects are not required to be correspondingly adjusted, though they may request one if desired.

continued on next page

---

[38]   Government of Ghana, Ghana Carbon Market Office. 2022. *Ghana's Framework on International Carbon Markets and Non-Market Approaches. Accra.*

Box 5 *continued*

Key Insights

As the experience of Ghana demonstrates, engagement in Article 6 is most likely to meet a country's strategic needs if it is informed by a long-term strategy for NDC achievement. This model may not necessarily work for all countries due to the differences in how the NDCs are designed, particularly concerning the delineation of sectors as conditional and unconditional, and the repercussions of defining eligible mitigation activities.

▶ PROCESSES AND INSTITUTIONAL ARRANGEMENTS FOR ASSESSING, GRANTING, OR DENYING AUTHORIZATION

Ghana Experience

The implementation of Ghana's Article 6 framework is led by the Ministry of Environment, Science, Technology, and Innovation. The ministry and the Environmental Protection Agency host the new Carbon Market Office. Ghana also established several new entities:

- Carbon Market Inter-Ministerial Committee
- Carbon Market Committee
- Carbon Market Technical Advisory Committee

Ghana shall issue a letter of authorization to eligible mitigation activities. Activities on the Ghana "whitelist" may receive pre-authorization by requesting a "Letter of Assurance" from the Carbon Market Office.

Key Insights

Ghana's Article 6 institutional arrangements led to the creation of several new offices.

As part of their Article 6 frameworks, countries will need to define the "letters" of intent, pre-authorization, authorization, etc. Multiple national agencies and ministries may need to be involved in the review and approval of authorization requests, and coordination between these entities structured with the intent to minimize administrative burden and duplication.

▶ MEASURES TO MITIGATE THE RISK OF OVERSELLING MITIGATION OUTCOMES

Ghana Experience

To reduce the risk of overselling mitigation outcomes, Ghana established safeguards and a national buffer system, reserving 1% of issued mitigation outcomes in a "National Buffer Account" to be used toward the NDC in the event of overselling or contributing to the overall mitigation of global emissions.

The Government of Indonesia took a similar approach, with national regulations on carbon pricing that include high-level provisions for the international transfer of carbon offsets. To minimize the risk of overselling, Indonesia established a "buffer reserve," with differentiated buffer obligations by use case:

- Domestic Offset: 0%–5% of the units
- International Offset: 10%–20% of the units; If outside NDC: At least 20% of the units

Key Insights

The primary approach to minimizing the risk of overselling is to establish and adhere to a long-term strategy for NDC achievement. However, to further reduce the risk of overselling mitigation outcomes and undermining NDC achievement, countries may wish to establish a national buffer account or carbon credit reserve.

Source: Asian Development Bank and Pollination.

4 Conclusion

In response to the Paris Agreement and the need to limit warming to 1.5 degrees Celsius, deep emission cuts are required across all sectors and regions, with residual emissions neutralized by carbon dioxide removals. Carbon markets provide mechanisms for countries to incentivize the reduction of their domestic emissions as well as a pathway to cooperate with other countries or non-state actors through the international transfer of mitigation outcomes under Article 6 of the Paris Agreement. As countries commit to increasingly more ambitious NDCs, many are considering how to leverage both domestic and international carbon markets and what impact their participation in carbon markets could have on their decarbonization pathway.

Countries can either create their domestic crediting schemes to generate carbon credits or adopt (and potentially adjust) international carbon credit standards. Credits generated within the borders of a country can be used for a variety of purposes depending on the country, including for domestic compliance use (e.g., a carbon tax or cap-and-trade system), international compliance use, or international or domestic voluntary use. VCMs are also growing rapidly as corporates seek to purchase carbon credits as part of their commitments to transition to net zero.

To assess the appropriate mix of carbon market policies, policymakers must define their objectives as well as understand the tradeoffs between various carbon market mechanisms. For example, policymakers will need to evaluate the benefits of selling mitigation outcomes today to attract much-needed carbon finance, against the need to meet their own increasingly ambitious NDC targets. Evaluating this tradeoff requires a long-term strategy to achieve the NDC that informs engagement with Article 6, including guiding principles and criteria for mitigation outcomes to be eligible for international transfer. Beyond strategic considerations, governments that wish to participate in carbon markets will be confronted with operational requirements and the need for new legal and policy frameworks as well as new reporting and accounting frameworks that underpin the integrity of the mitigation outcomes traded.

Countries across Asia and the Pacific and globally are working through these strategic choices with a view to how international carbon markets fit within their long-term decarbonization plan. The aim is to assist countries that have indicated a willingness to participate in carbon markets to operationalize their carbon market strategies and begin building the policy, regulatory, and institutional infrastructure.

APPENDIX 1
Prerequisites for International Cooperation under Articles 6.2 and 6.4

Participation in international cooperation under Articles 6.2 and 6.4 of the Paris Agreement requires that participating parties fulfill several prerequisites. Many of these prerequisites are addressed as part of a country's Article 6 readiness activities.

Party Eligibility under Article 6

The party will need to ensure it is eligible to participate in Article 6, as per the requirements of Decision 2/CMA.3 and Decision 3/CMA.3 (Box A1.1).

Box A1.1: Party Eligibility under Article 6

For Article 6.2, each participating party shall ensure that:

(i) Its participation in the cooperative approach and the authorization, transfer, and use of internationally transferred mitigation outcomes (ITMOs) is consistent with Decision 2/CMA.3 and other decisions of the Conference of the Parties serving as the meeting of the Parties to the Paris Agreement (CMA);

(ii) It is a party to the Paris Agreement;

(iii) It has prepared, communicated, and is maintaining a nationally determined contribution (NDC);

(iv) It has arrangements in place for authorizing the use of ITMOs toward the achievement of NDCs;

(v) It has arrangements in place that are consistent with Decision 2/CMA.3 and other CMA decisions for tracking ITMOs;

(vi) It has provided the most recent national inventory report required following decision 18/CMA.1; and

(vii) Its participation contributes to the implementation of its NDC and long-term low-emission development strategy, if it has submitted one, and the long-term goals of the Paris Agreement.

Source: United Nations Framework Convention on Climate Change (UNFCCC), Conference of the Parties serving as the meeting of the Parties to the Paris Agreement (CMA). 2021. Decision 2/CMA.3, Part II, paras. 3–5.

For Article 6.4 participation, each host party shall ensure that:

(i) It is a party to the Paris Agreement;

(ii) It has prepared, communicated, and is maintaining an NDC;

(iii) It has indicated publicly to the Supervisory Body how its participation in the mechanism contributes to sustainable development while acknowledging that the consideration of sustainable development is a national prerogative; and

(iv) It has indicated publicly to the Supervisory Body the types of Article 6.4 activity that it would consider approving and how such types of activity and any associated emission reductions would contribute to the achievement of its NDC, if applicable, its long-term low greenhouse gas emission development strategy, if it has submitted one, and the long-term goals of the Paris Agreement.

Source: UNFCCC, CMA. 2021. Decision 3/CMA.3. Part IV, para. 26.

Activity Eligibility under Article 6

After confirming whether the party is eligible to participate in international cooperation under Article 6, the parties involved will then need to determine whether the mitigation activity is eligible for either Article 6.2 or 6.4 (Box A1.2).

Box A1.2: Activity Eligibility under Article 6

For Article 6.2 purposes, internationally transferred mitigation outcomes (ITMOs) are:

   (i)   real, verified, and additional;

   (ii)   emission reductions and removals, including mitigation co-benefits resulting from adaptation actions and/or economic diversification plans or the means to achieve them, when internationally transferred;

   (iii) measured in metric tons of carbon dioxide equivalent following the methodologies and metrics assessed by the Intergovernmental Panel on Climate Change and adopted by the meeting of the Parties to the Paris Agreement (CMA) or in other non-greenhouse gas (GHG) metrics determined by the participating parties that are consistent with the nationally determined contributions (NDCs) of the participating parties;

   (iv) from a cooperative approach referred to in Article 6.2, that involves the international transfer of mitigation outcomes authorized for use toward an NDC under Article 6.3;

   (v)   generated in respect of or representing mitigation from 2021 onwards;

   (vi) mitigation outcomes authorized by a participating party for use for international mitigation purposes other than the achievement of an NDC or authorized for other purposes as determined by the first transferring participating party; and

   (vii) Article 6.4 emission reductions issued under the mechanism established by Article 6.4, when they are authorized for use toward the achievement of NDCs and/or authorized for use for other international mitigation purposes.

Source: United Nations Framework Convention on Climate Change (UNFCCC), Conference of the Parties serving as the meeting of the Parties to the Paris Agreement (CMA). 2021. Decision 2/CMA.3. Part I, para. 1.

To be eligible under Article 6.4, the activity

   (i)   shall be designed to achieve mitigation of GHG emissions that are additional, including reducing emissions, increasing removals and mitigation co-benefits of adaptation actions and/or economic diversification plans ("emission reductions"), and not lead to an increase in global emissions;

   (ii)   may be a project, program of activities, or other type of activity approved by the Supervisory Body;

   (iii) shall be designed to achieve emission reductions in the host party;

   (iv) shall deliver real, measurable, and long-term benefits related to climate change;

   (v)   shall minimize the risk of non-permanence of emission reductions over multiple NDC implementation periods and, where reversals occur, ensure that these are addressed in full;

   (vi) shall minimize the risk of leakage and adjust for any remaining leakage in the calculation of emission reductions or removals;

   (vii) shall minimize and, where possible, avoid negative environmental and social impacts;

   (viii) shall undergo local and, where appropriate, subnational stakeholder consultation consistent with applicable domestic arrangements concerning public participation and local communities and indigenous peoples, as applicable;

   (ix) shall apply a crediting period for the issuance of A6.4ERs that is a maximum of 5 years renewable a maximum of twice, or a maximum of 10 years with no option of renewal, that is appropriate to the activity, or, in respect of activities involving removals, a crediting period of a maximum of 15 years renewable a maximum of twice that is appropriate to the activity, and that is subject to approval by the Supervisory Body, or any shorter crediting period specified by the host party; the crediting period shall not start before 2021; and

   (x)   shall apply a mechanism methodology that has been developed following Decision 3/CMA.3 and approved by the Supervisory Body.

Source: UNFCCC, CMA. 2021. Decision 3/CMA.3. Part V.A., paras. 31–32.

APPENDIX 2
Legal and Institutional Requirements to Authorize Mitigation Outcomes under Articles 6.2 and 6.4 for International Transfer

Article 6.2

While Article 6.2 guidance establishes the requirement that mitigation outcomes be authorized for international use and transfer by the host country, the guidance provides little information on how such authorization should be expressed or documented. The draft annual information reporting template does however provide the following minimum authorization requirements:[1]

(i)   date of authorization by the first transferring party;

(ii) authorization ID as assigned by the first transferring party, and may include a link to the public evidence of authorization by the first transferring party;

(iii) purposes for authorization that include "nationally determined contribution" (NDC), "other international mitigation purposes," or "NDC and other international mitigation purposes;"

(iv) when applicable, the other international mitigation purposes authorized by the party; and

(v)   if other international mitigation purposes are authorized, the first transferring participating party's definition of "first transfer" (as per decision 2/CMA.3, annex, para. 2[b]).

At the 27th Conference of the Parties (COP27), many authorization decisions were deferred for consideration and adoption at the next COP, following further work from the Subsidiary Body for Scientific and Technological Advice, including the process for authorization and, notably, the scope of changes to authorization for use of internationally transferred mitigation outcomes (ITMOs).[2]

Ultimately, the approach to authorization of each country may be different to accommodate their individualized needs and context.

Processes for the authorization of ITMOs will require three core elements:

(i)   Processes to determine eligibility for authorization.

Countries will require clear criteria for the eligibility of mitigation outcomes for international transfer under Article 6.2. Countries may decide to pre-authorize or exclude certain categories of mitigation outcomes for international transfer. Pre-authorization would involve indications from a host country that mitigation outcomes from a particular mitigation activity (or category of mitigation activity, or sector) are aligned with nationally determined eligibility criteria, and that the mitigation outcomes from the eligible activity could be authorized upon meeting subsequent requirements.[3] Pre-authorization may encourage

---

1   United Nations Framework Convention on Climate Change (UNFCCC), Conference of the Parties serving as the meeting of the Parties to the Paris Agreement (CMA). 2022. Decision 6/CMA.4, Matters Relating to Cooperative Approaches referred to in Article 6, paragraph 2, of the Paris Agreement. Annex VII.

2   UNFCCC, CMA. 2022. Decision 6/CMA.4, Matters Relating to Cooperative Approaches referred to in Article 6, paragraph 2, of the Paris Agreement. para. 17.

3   Organisation for Economic Co-operation and Development (OECD) and International Energy Agency (IEA). 2022. *The Birth of an ITMO: Authorisation under Article 6 of the Paris Agreement*. p. 34.

the private sector to invest in pre-authorized mitigation activities. Pre-authorization could take several forms, including a letter of assurance or intent (footnote 3).

(ii)   Processes and institutional arrangements for assessing, granting, denying, and communicating authorization.

Countries must determine which entity or entities will be involved in the review and, if applicable, approval of authorization requests as well as the steps and timelines for this process. Ideally, authorization processes established by countries will be on the public record and provide transparency on the authorization process to both the sellers and purchasers of mitigation outcomes.

(iii)   Establish arrangements for tracking ITMOs and applying corresponding adjustments.

Countries must have arrangements in place for tracking ITMOs.

Article 6.4

Institutional Capacity to Fulfil Article 6.4 Participation Requirements

Countries will need to ensure they have the institutional capacity to fulfill the participation requirements for the Article 6.4 mechanism.

Institutional Capacity and Procedures to Support the Approval and Registration of Article 6.4 Activities and Authorization

For mitigation activities to be considered Article 6.4 activities, they must meet certain requirements, including concerning stakeholder engagement.[4] Article 6.4 activities must follow mechanism methodologies, which can be developed by activity participants, host countries, stakeholders, or the Supervisory Body, and must be approved by the Supervisory Body.[5] Countries must provide the Supervisory Body with approval of the activity, before a registration request.[6] Countries will also need to approve the renewal of crediting periods if the country intends to allow the activity to continue beyond the first crediting period (footnote 7).

Host counties must provide the Supervisory Body with authorization of public or private entities to participate in the activity as activity participants under the mechanism (footnote 7). Host countries must also provide a statement to the Supervisory Body specifying whether it authorizes A6.4ERs issued for the activity for use toward the achievement of NDCs and/or for other international mitigation purposes.[7] At COP27, it was agreed that the Subsidiary Body for Scientific and Technological Advice continue its consideration of the form and timing of the authorization statement.[8]

---

[4]   UNFCCC, CMA. 2021. Decision 3/CMA.3, Rules, Modalities and Procedures for the Mechanism Established by Article 6, paragraph 4, of the Paris Agreement, Chapter V; UNFCCC, CMA. 2022. Decision 7/CMA.4, Guidance on the Mechanism Established by Article 6, paragraph 4, of the Paris Agreement. para. 9(c).
[5]   UNFCCC, CMA. 2021. Decision 3/CMA.3, Rules, Modalities and Procedures for the Mechanism Established by Article 6, paragraph 4, of the Paris Agreement. Chapter V, B.
[6]   UNFCCC, CMA. 2021, Decision 3/CMA.3, Rules, Modalities and Procedures for the Mechanism Established by Article 6, paragraph 4, of the Paris Agreement. Chapter V, C.
[7]   UNFCCC, CMA. 2021. Decision 3/CMA.3, Rules, Modalities and Procedures for the Mechanism Established by Article 6, paragraph 4, of the Paris Agreement. Chapter V, C; UNFCCC, CMA. 2022. Decision 7/CMA.4, Guidance on the Mechanism Established by Article 6, paragraph 4, of the Paris Agreement. Annex I, para. 26.
[8]   UNFCCC, CMA. 2022. Decision 7/CMA.4, Guidance on the Mechanism Established by Article 6, paragraph 4, of the Paris Agreement. para. 9(c).

Processes for Applying Corresponding Adjustments to Authorized A6.4ERs

At COP27, parties agreed that the Article 6.4 mechanism registry shall track A6.4ERs that are:

Authorized toward the achievement of an acquiring country's NDC or for other international mitigation purposes, known as Authorized A6.4ERs;[9] or

Not authorized for use toward the achievement of an NDC or other international mitigation purposes, known as Mitigation Contribution A6.4ERs.[10]

Host countries who authorize A6.4ERs for use toward the achievement of NDCs and/or for other international mitigation purposes must apply the corresponding adjustments.

Accounting and Reporting Infrastructure to Support Article 6

Boxes A2.1, A2.2, A2.3, and A2.4 for an overview of the accounting and reporting infrastructure available under Article 6 and the related obligations of parties as outlined in the guidance and rules adopted by CMA 3 and CMA 4 (footnote 10).

Box A2.1 Centralized Accounting and Reporting Platform

The secretariat shall establish and maintain a CARP as a digital web-based platform for publishing nonconfidential information submitted by participating parties under their reporting requirements.

As part of administering the CARP, the secretariat will provide an annual report to the CMA on party activities under Article 6.2, including recorded ITMOs, corresponding adjustments, and emissions balances.

Reports generated by the Article 6 technical expert review team will also be made publicly available on the CARP.

At COP27, parties requested that the secretariat make a test version of the CARP available by June 2024, with a view to the first version being finalized by June 2025. Parties also requested that the secretariat provide an interim solution by January 2023 for the submission of reporting information by parties until the CARP and Article 6 database are released.

Party obligations

Comply with reporting requirements.

_____

CARP = centralized accounting and reporting platform, COP27 = 27th Conference of the Parties, CMA = Conference of the Parties serving as the meeting of the Parties to the Paris Agreement, ITMO = internationally transferred mitigation outcomes.

Source: United Nations Framework Convention on Climate Change.

---

9   UNFCCC, CMA. 2022. Decision 7/CMA.4, Guidance on the Mechanism Established by Article 6, paragraph 4, of the Paris Agreement. Annex I, para. 29.
10 UNFCCC, CMA. 2021. Decision 2/CMA.3, Guidance on Cooperative Approaches Referred to in Article 6, paragraph 2, of the Paris Agreement. Annex, Chapter VI; UNFCCC, CMA. 2022. Decision 6/CMA.4, Matters Relating to Cooperative Approaches Referred to in Article 6, paragraph 2, of the Paris Agreement. Annex I, Chapter II; Chapter III.

Box A2.2: Article 6 Database

The secretariat will implement an Article 6 database as an integrated but distinct database within the centralized accounting and recording platform to enable the recording of corresponding adjustments and emissions balances and information on internationally transferred mitigation outcomes (ITMOs) first transferred, transferred, acquired, held, canceled, canceled for overall mitigation in global emissions if any, and/or used by participating parties.

The database will identify ITMOs by unique identifiers that distinguish, at a minimum, the participating party, vintage of underlying mitigation, activity type, and sector(s).

The Article 6 database will be designed to enable the identification of any inconsistencies, allowing the relevant parties to be notified.

Party obligations:

Comply with reporting requirements.

Source: United Nations Framework Convention on Climate Change.

Box A2.3: National Registry or International Registry

Parties must have, or have access to, a registry for tracking and shall ensure that such registry records, as applicable, the following items: "authorization, first transfer, transfer, acquisition, use towards NDCs, authorization for use towards other international mitigation purposes, and voluntary cancellation (including for overall mitigation in global emissions, if applicable), and shall have accounts as necessary."[a]

The secretariat will implement an international registry for participating parties that do not have or do not have access to a registry. The international registry shall, to track and record ITMOs, comprise an electronic database and other technical and administrative arrangements, supporting accounts for each participating party.

At COP27, parties requested that the Subsidiary Body for Scientific and Technological Advice and the secretariat further develop certain aspects of the international registry, providing an interim solution for participating parties until the international registry becomes operational.

This international registry will form part of the centralized accounting and reporting platform.

A participating party may connect its registry to the international registry.

Party obligations:

Establish a national registry capable of recording the above items; or

Request an account in the international registry.

Note that the international registry administrator shall assist the least-developed countries and small island developing states that use the international registry with functions and processes, as necessary, subject to the availability of financial resources.

COP27 = 27th Conference of the Parties, ITMO = internationally transferred mitigation outcome, NDC = nationally determined contribution.

[a] United Nations Framework Convention on Climate Change, Conference of the Parties serving as the meeting of the Parties to the Paris Agreement. 2022. Decision 6/CMA.4, Matters Relating to Cooperative Approaches referred to in Article 6, paragraph 2, of the Paris Agreement. Annex VII.

Source: United Nations Framework Convention on Climate Change.

Box A2.4: Article 6.4 Mechanism Registry

The Supervisory Body for the Article 6.4 mechanism will establish a registry for the mechanism. The secretariat will serve as the mechanism registry administrator, maintaining and operating the registry under the supervision of the Supervisory Body.

The mechanism registry will take the form of a standardized electronic database and shall track A6.4ERs and CERs transferred to the mechanism registry.

The mechanism registry shall perform issuance, forwarding, first transfer, transfer, cancellation, voluntary cancellation, and retirement of A6.4ERs or, where applicable, of CERs transferred to the mechanism registry.

The mechanism registry will contain at least a pending account, holding account, retirement account, cancellation account, account for cancellation toward overall mitigation in global emissions, and a share of proceeds for adaptation account, as well as a holding account for each party and certain public or private entities, as authorized by a party.

The mechanism registry shall be connected to the international registry referred to above.

The mechanism registry shall distinguish A6.4ERs that are authorized for use toward the achievement of NDCs and/or for use for other international mitigation purposes.

The mechanism registry administrator will implement the levies to the Adaptation Fund and buffer to deliver overall mitigation of global emissions.

Party obligations:

Apply for a holding account.

Ensure compliance with the processes outlined in Article 6.4 in Chapter 2, including, in particular, providing a statement to the Supervisory Body specifying whether it authorizes A6.4ERs issued for the activity for use toward the achievement of NDCs and/or for other international mitigation purposes.

_____

A6.4ER = Article 6.4 Emission Reduction Unit, CER = certified emission reduction, NDC = nationally determined contribution.
Source: United Nations Framework Convention on Climate Change.

International Transparency and Reporting Infrastructure

Parties who engage in cooperative approaches under Article 6 are subject to several reporting requirements. Information submitted by a party under these reporting requirements that is not identified by that party as confidential shall be made public on the CARP.[11]

_____

[11]   UNFCCC, CMA. 2021. Decision 2/CMA.3, Guidance on Cooperative Approaches Referred to in Article 6, paragraph 2, of the Paris Agreement. Annex, para. 24.

Article 6.2 Initial Report

Each participating party must submit an Article 6.2 initial report. This report is to be submitted no later than the authorization of ITMOs from a cooperative approach or where practical (in the view of the participating party) in conjunction with the next biennial transparency report due for the period of NDC implementation.[12] Parties agreed upon the outline of the initial report at COP27 in *Annex V, Outline for the initial report and updated initial report referred to in decision 2/CMA.3, annex, chapter IV.A (Initial report)* of the COP27 decision regarding Article 6.2.[13]

This outline will require participating parties to report against four key categories of information:

(i)   Participation responsibilities required under the guidance of Article 6.2;

(ii)   Information relating to the party's NDC and the intention to use cooperative approaches that involve the use of ITMOs under Article 6 toward NDCs;

(iii)   Information on ITMO metrics, method for applying corresponding adjustments, and method for quantification of the NDC;

(iv)   Information on each cooperative approach including authorization and integrity considerations. Note that this information must be provided in the initial report and updated initial report for each cooperative approach separately.

Annual Information—Article 6.2

Participating parties must provide information on their carbon market activities on an annual basis, no later than 15 April of the following year in an agreed electronic format. This information will be recorded in the Article 6 database.[14]

Parties agreed upon a draft version of the agreed electronic format of this annual information at COP27 in *Annex VII, Draft version of the agreed electronic format referred to in decision 2/CMA.3, annex, chapter IV.B (Annual information)* of the COP27 decision regarding Article 6.2.[15]

This draft format sets out tables covering participating party actions and holdings. These will require participating parties to provide information regarding the following:

(i)   the relevant cooperative approach;

(ii)   the ITMOs unique identifier;

(iii)   the metric and quantity of ITMOs;

(iv)   ITMO details including the first transferring party, vintage, sector, and activity type;

(v)   authorization, including the purposes for which authorization has been given;

(vi)   the first transferring party's definition or "first transfer;" and

(vii) various action details including the transferring participating party, acquiring participating party, purposes for cancellation, using a participating party or authorized entity or entities, and first transfer.

---

[12]   UNFCCC, CMA. 2021. Decision 2/CMA.3, Guidance on Cooperative Approaches Referred to in Article 6, paragraph 2, of the Paris Agreement. Annex, para. 18.

[13]   UNFCCC, CMA. 2022. Decision 6/CMA.4, Matters Relating to Cooperative Approaches referred to in Article 6, paragraph 2, of the Paris Agreement.

[14]   UNFCCC, CMA. 2021. Decision 2/CMA.3, Guidance on Cooperative Approaches Referred to in Article 6, paragraph 2, of the Paris Agreement. Annex, Chapter IV, B.

[15]   UNFCCC, CMA. 2022. Decision 6/CMA.4, Matters Relating to Cooperative Approaches referred to in Article 6, paragraph 2, of the Paris Agreement.

Regular Information—Article 6.2

Every 2 years, parties must submit a biennial transparency report (BTR). As an annex to the BTR, parties are required to submit regular information on their participation in cooperative approaches no later than 31 December of the relevant year.[16]

Parties agreed upon an outline for this regular information at COP27 in *Annex VI, Outline for annex 4 (Information in relation to the Party's participation in cooperative approaches, as applicable)* to the biennial transparency report, as referred to in decision 2/CMA.3, annex, chapter IV.C (Regular information), paragraphs 21–22 of the COP27 decision on Article 6.2.[17]

This outline will require participating parties to provide regular information across the following key categories of information:

(i) participation responsibilities;

(ii) updates to the information provided by the party in its initial report and any previous BTRs;

(iii) authorizations including information on its authorization(s) of use of ITMOs toward the achievement of NDCs and authorization for use for other international mitigation purposes, including any changes to earlier authorizations;

(iv) corresponding adjustments, including integrity aspects (i.e., how double counting is avoided, how corresponding adjustments ensure that participation in cooperative approaches does not lead to a net increase in emissions across participating parties within and between NDC implementation periods);

(v) information on how the party has ensured that ITMOs that have been used toward achievement of its NDC or mitigation outcome(s) authorized for use and that have been used for other international mitigation purposes will not be further transferred, further canceled, or otherwise used; and

(vi) information on each cooperative approach. Note that the information required must be provided for each cooperative approach.

Reporting to the Supervisory Body – Article 6.4

Host parties must provide the Supervisory Body with information regarding their participation responsibilities as set out in paragraphs 26–28 of the rules, modalities, and procedures agreed for Article 6.4 at COP26.[18] Parties agreed at COP27 that the Supervisory Body shall promptly make the received information publicly available on the UNFCCC website.[19]

Technical Expert Review

The information submitted by countries will be subject to an Article 6 technical expert review following guidelines adopted by the CMA.[20] Those guidelines were agreed at COP27 in Annex II, *Guidelines for the Article 6 technical expert review pursuant to decision 2/CMA.3, annex, chapter V (Review).*[21]

---

[16] UNFCCC, CMA. 2021. Decision 2/CMA.3, Guidance on Cooperative Approaches Referred to in Article 6, paragraph 2, of the Paris Agreement. Annex, para. 21.

[17] UNFCCC, CMA. 2022. Decision 6/CMA.4, Matters Relating to Cooperative Approaches Referred to in Article 6, paragraph 2, of the Paris Agreement.

[18] UNFCCC, CMA. 2021. Decision 3/CMA.3, Rules, Modalities and Procedures for the Mechanism Established by Article 6, paragraph 4, of the Paris Agreement. Annex, paras. 26–28.

[19] UNFCCC, CMA. 2022. Decision 7/CMA.4, Guidance on the Mechanism Established by Article 6, paragraph 4, of the Paris Agreement. Annex I, para. 25.

[20] UNFCCC, CMA. 2021. Decision 2/CMA.3, Guidance on Cooperative Approaches Referred to in Article 6, paragraph 2, of the Paris Agreement. Annex, paras. 25–26.

[21] UNFCCC, CMA. 2022. Decision 6/CMA.4, Matters Relating to Cooperative Approaches Referred to in Article 6, paragraph 2, of the Paris Agreement.

The technical expert review is intended to, among other things, promote transparency, accuracy, completeness, consistency, and comparability, and facilitate the application of robust accounting for engagement in cooperative approaches under Article 6.2.[22]

The technical expert review will encompass:[23]

(i)   The initial report and updated initial report submitted by each participating party;

(ii)   Regular information, as an annex to a BTR, submitted by each participating party; and

(iii) The results of the consistency check performed by the secretariat on the information submitted by the participating party for recording in the Article 6 database.

The Article 6 technical expert review team shall prepare a report on its review that will, if applicable, include recommendations to the participating country on how to improve consistency with the guidance on Article 6.2 and relevant decisions. Parties agreed on an outline of that report at COP27 in *Annex III, Outline of the Article 6 technical expert review report of the decision on Article 6.2.*[24] Reports of the Article 6 technical expert review team will be made publicly available on the CARP.[25]

Article 6.2: Processes for the Application of Corresponding Adjustments

Applying Corresponding Adjustments

Several factors will influence the application of corresponding adjustments by participating parties.

Type of Nationally Determined Contribution Target

Countries can set and express targets in their NDCs in a range of ways, including absolute emissions targets, relative emissions targets, intensity emissions targets, and non-GHG targets.

Targets can also be expressed as multiyear targets or single-year targets.

To underpin the implementation of corresponding adjustments, countries must ensure there is clarity in the mitigation outcomes covered by each target in their NDCs and the nature of those targets.

Timing of Corresponding Adjustments

The timing of corresponding adjustments is complex and will depend upon whether a country has a multiyear or single-year NDC target.

---

[22] UNFCCC, CMA. 2022. Decision 6/CMA.4, Matters Relating to Cooperative Approaches Referred to in Article 6, paragraph 2, of the Paris Agreement. Annex II, para. 1.

[23] UNFCCC, CMA. 2022. Decision 6/CMA.4, Matters Relating to Cooperative Approaches Referred to in Article 6, paragraph 2, of the Paris Agreement. para. 11.

[24] UNFCCC, CMA. 2022. Decision 6/CMA.4, Matters Relating to Cooperative Approaches Referred to in Article 6, paragraph 2, of the Paris Agreement. Annex III.

[25] UNFCCC, CMA. 2022. Decision 6/CMA.4, Matters Relating to Cooperative Approaches Referred to in Article 6, paragraph 2, of the Paris Agreement. Annex II, para. 21.

Multiyear NDC target. In the event a country maintains a multiyear NDC target (e.g., a target capturing 2021 through 2030), it would apply a corresponding adjustment on an annual basis equivalent to the ITMOs "first transferred" in the case of a seller country, and "used" in the case of the buyer country and report such corresponding adjustments in its annual report submitted to the Article 6 database. It would then further elaborate on such reported transfers and corresponding adjustments in its BTR.

(i)   Single-year NDC target. Parties may choose between two approaches when reporting their Article 6 transfers under an NDC that reflects its target as a single-year target (e.g., a 2030 target): the trajectory approach or the averaging approach.

(ii)   Trajectory approach. If a party uses a trajectory approach, the application of corresponding adjustments replicates that of the multi-year NDC target described above. A corresponding adjustment for ITMOs first transferred and used would be required to be made on an annual basis in the Article 6 database.

(iii)   Averaging approach. If a party uses an averaging approach, it will apply an indicative corresponding adjustment on an annual basis in the Article 6 database in the years before the NDC target year. In the NDC target year, the party would apply a corresponding adjustment in the amount of the average annual ITMOs transferred over the entire period.

At COP27, countries deferred a decision on the elaboration of further guidance concerning corresponding adjustments for multiyear or single-year NDCs, including the methods for establishing an indicative trajectory and the methods for demonstrating the representativeness of averaging.[26]

Application of Corresponding Adjustment

Following the selection of an appropriate accounting approach, the host country must apply corresponding adjustments by:[27]

(i)   adding the quantity of ITMOs authorized and first transferred, for the calendar year in which the mitigation outcomes occurred; and

(ii)   subtracting the number of ITMOs used for the calendar year in which the mitigation outcomes are used toward the implementation and achievement of the NDC, ensuring that the mitigation outcomes are used within the same NDC implementation period as when they occurred.

Corresponding adjustments are also required for ITMOs traded in non-greenhouse gas metrics.[28]

Reporting Corresponding Adjustments

As a part of Article 6.2 reporting requirements, participating parties must report on the method for corresponding adjustments applied throughout the NDC implementation period in their initial reports and regular information submitted as an annex to the BTR.[29]

---

[26]   UNFCCC, CMA. 2022. Decision 6/CMA.4, Matters Relating to Cooperative Approaches Referred to in Article 6, paragraph 2, of the Paris Agreement. Annex II, para. 16.

[27]   UNFCCC, CMA. 2021. Decision 2/CMA.3, Guidance on Cooperative Approaches Referred to in Article 6, paragraph 2, of the Paris Agreement. Annex, para. 8.

[28]   UNFCCC, CMA. 2021. Decision 2/CMA.3, Guidance on Cooperative Approaches Referred to in Article 6, paragraph 2, of the Paris Agreement. Annex, para. 9.

[29]   UNFCCC, CMA. 2021. Decision 2/CMA.3, Guidance on Cooperative Approaches Referred to in Article 6, paragraph 2, of the Paris Agreement. Annex, para. 22.

Glossary

Article 6	Article 6 of the Paris Agreement provides the overarching global framework for voluntary cooperation among parties in the implementation of their nationally determined contributions (NDCs) to allow for higher climate mitigation and adaptation ambition through market-based and nonmarket-based measures.
Article 6 guidance and rules	Decisions on Article 6 at the 26th United Nations Climate Change Conference of the Parties (COP26) adopted guidance on cooperative approaches referred to in Article 6.2;[a] rules, modalities, and procedures for the mechanism established by Article 6.4; and a work program under the framework for nonmarket approaches under Article 6.8.[b] As this paper primarily focuses on Articles 6.2 and 6.4, the authors use the unofficial phrase "Article 6 guidance and rules" to encompass the decisions on both Article 6.2 and Article 6.4.
Authorized A6.4ERs	Units under the Article 6.4 mechanism, Article 6.4 Emission Reductions (A6.4ERs) are authorized for use toward the achievement of NDCs and/or for other international mitigation purposes (following the guidance for Article 6.2). This term was introduced as part of the COP27 decision on the rules, modalities, and procedures for the mechanism established by Article 6.4.[c]
Carbon credit	A discrete unit representing a specific amount of emission reductions or removals of greenhouse gas, usually expressed in terms of metric tons of carbon dioxide equivalent (tCO_2e). Carbon credits are often issued, tracked, and canceled on registries and may have unique identifiers such as serial numbers.
Carbon crediting scheme	A scheme (voluntary or compliance-based) managed by a central organization that registers climate-change mitigation activities and issues carbon credits for the emission reductions achieved by those activities. Generally, carbon crediting schemes can be international and governed by climate treaties (e.g., Clean Development Mechanism); independently governed, or governed by third-party organizations (e.g., Gold Standard or Verra); or they can be regional, domestic, and subnational crediting mechanisms that are governed by their respective jurisdictional governing bodies.
Carbon markets	The global trading of both compliance-based and voluntary units that represent an allowance to emit (such as under the EU emissions trading system) or carbon credits.
Co-benefits	Non-carbon social and environmental benefits arising from mitigation activities.
Corresponding adjustment	An accounting method to be applied to a national emissions balance due to the use and international transfer of internationally transferred mitigation outcomes (ITMOs) and A6.4ERs within the context of Article 6 of the Paris Agreement to avoid double counting. A corresponding adjustment is applied to ensure that the host country does not use the volume of emission reductions or removals that are transferred to another party for its own NDC achievement, which would constitute double counting. Corresponding adjustments may also be made by host countries when emission reductions or removals are transferred to non-party entities to avoid double claiming. Host countries may decide whether to authorize emission reductions or removals as ITMOs— including the export of A6.4ERs—and apply a corresponding adjustment, including for voluntary markets.

continued on next page

Glossary *continued*

Double claiming	Where the same emission reduction or removal is claimed by two stakeholders (e.g., a corporation and a country) toward achieving mitigation targets or goals.
Double counting	Where the same emission reduction or removal is accounted for by two or more countries toward achieving mitigation targets or goals under the same program (e.g., two countries using the same emission reduction or removal for compliance under the Paris Agreement).
Emissions reduction	Greenhouse gas (GHG) abatement resulting from mitigation activities.
Emissions removal	GHG abatement resulting from activities that remove GHGs from the atmosphere by technical or biological means and store it in geological, biological, or ocean reservoirs, or products.
Internationally transferred mitigation outcomes (ITMOs)	Emission reductions or removals resulting from mitigation activities under Article 6.2 of the Paris Agreement and authorized by parties for use toward NDCs or "other international mitigation purposes." Following the guidance on cooperative approaches, ITMOs are real, verified, and additional emission reductions or removals generated from 2021 onward and transferred between countries for use toward their NDC commitments and other international mitigation purposes. [d]
Mitigation activity	An activity that delivers a reduction of GHG emissions from sources or removal by sinks, that accumulate and store carbon for an indefinite period and thereby removes carbon dioxide from the atmosphere.
Mitigation contribution A6.4ERs	Units under the Article 6.4 mechanism (A6.4ERs) not specified as authorized for use toward the achievement of NDCs and/or for other international mitigation purposes, which may be used, among other things, for results-based climate finance, domestic mitigation pricing schemes, or domestic price-based measures, to contribute to the reduction of emission levels in the host party. This term was introduced as part of the COP27 decision on the rules, modalities, and procedures for the mechanism established by Article 6.4. [e]
Mitigation outcome	Units denominated as carbon dioxide equivalent that represent GHG emission reductions or removals.
Other international mitigation purposes	As well as for use toward NDCs, ITMOs can be authorized and transferred for use toward "other international mitigation purposes," which encompass both "international mitigation purposes" (e.g., use toward an international compliance obligation such as the Carbon Offsetting and Reduction Scheme for International Aviation or CORSIA) and "other purposes as determined by the first transferring participating Party" (also known as "other purposes").
Paris Agreement	The Paris Agreement is a legally binding international treaty on climate change with the overarching goal to hold the increase in the global average temperature to well below 2°Celsius above pre-industrial levels and pursue efforts to limit the temperature increase to 1.5°Celsius above pre-industrial levels.
Party	A country that is a signatory to an international agreement such as the United Nations Framework Convention on Climate Change (UNFCCC) or the Paris Agreement.

[a] United Nations Framework Convention on Climate Change (UNFCCC), Conference of the Parties serving as the meeting of the Parties to the Paris Agreement (CMA). 2021. Decision 2/CMA.3, Guidance on cooperative approaches referred to in Article 6, paragraph 2, of the Paris Agreement; and UNFCCC, CMA. 2022. Decision 6/CMA.4, Matters relating to cooperative approaches referred to in Article 6, paragraph 2, of the Paris Agreement.

[b] UNFCCC, CMA. 2021. Decision 3/CMA.3, Rules, modalities and procedures for the mechanism established by Article 6, paragraph 4, of the Paris Agreement; and UNFCCC, CMA. 2022. Decision 7/CMA.4, Guidance on the mechanism established by Article 6, paragraph 4, of the Paris Agreement.

[c] UNFCCC, CMA. 2022. Decision 7/CMA.4, Guidance on the mechanism established by Article 6, paragraph 4, of the Paris Agreement. Annex I, para. 29.

[d] UNFCCC, CMA. 2021. Decision 2/CMA.3, Guidance on cooperative approaches referred to in Article 6, paragraph 2, of the Paris Agreement.

[e] UNFCCC, CMA. 2022. Decision 7/CMA.4, Guidance on the mechanism established by Article 6, paragraph 4, of the Paris Agreement. Annex I, para. 29.

www.ingramcontent.com/pod-product-compliance
Lightning Source LLC
Chambersburg PA
CBHW042035220326
41599CB00045BA/7402